S. Hrg. 113–477

HIGH FREQUENCY TRADING'S IMPACT ON THE ECONOMY

HEARING

BEFORE THE

SUBCOMMITTEE ON
SECURITIES, INSURANCE, AND INVESTMENT

OF THE

COMMITTEE ON
BANKING, HOUSING, AND URBAN AFFAIRS
UNITED STATES SENATE

ONE HUNDRED THIRTEENTH CONGRESS

SECOND SESSION

ON

EXAMINING THE VALUE, BENEFITS, RISKS, BURDENS, AND CONCERNS HIGH FREQUENCY TRADING CREATES FOR THE ECONOMY AND THE MARKETPLACE

JUNE 18, 2014

Printed for the use of the Committee on Banking, Housing, and Urban Affairs

Available at: http://www.fdsys.gov/

U.S. GOVERNMENT PRINTING OFFICE

91–299 PDF   WASHINGTON : 2014

For sale by the Superintendent of Documents, U.S. Government Printing Office
Internet: bookstore.gpo.gov   Phone: toll free (866) 512–1800; DC area (202) 512–1800
Fax: (202) 512–2104   Mail: Stop IDCC, Washington, DC 20402–0001

(II)

C O N T E N T S

WEDNESDAY, JUNE 18, 2014

WITNESSES

ADDITIONAL MATERIAL SUPPLIED FOR THE RECORD

(III)

HIGH FREQUENCY TRADING'S IMPACT ON THE ECONOMY

WEDNESDAY, JUNE 18, 2014

U.S. SENATE,
SUBCOMMITTEE ON SECURITIES, INSURANCE, AND
INVESTMENT,
COMMITTEE ON BANKING, HOUSING, AND URBAN AFFAIRS,
Washington, DC.

The Subcommittee met at 10:01 a.m., in room 538, Dirksen Senate Office Building, Hon. Mark R. Warner, Chairman of the Subcommittee, presiding.

OPENING STATEMENT OF CHAIRMAN MARK R. WARNER

Chairman WARNER. This hearing will come to order.

I want to thank Senator Johanns' staff for working with our office today in putting together today's hearings. I want to thank our witnesses, who I will come to introduce in a couple of moments.

I do feel, as I was mentioning a little bit yesterday, this is not the first hearing or even the first hearing this week on this subject. We perhaps were front-run a little bit yesterday by Senator Levin's activities, but we think we can build upon his good work as the Senate takes a look at this very important issue.

Yesterday, Senator Levin's hearing really focused on potential conflicts of interest between brokers and investors. Our hope will be that this hearing will take a larger, macro view of the effects of high frequency trading on the economy and the marketplace.

Over the past few decades, we have seen remarkable technological progress and innovation in our securities markets coupled with substantial regulatory reform. Now, some of these advances and reforms, including decimalization, have brought considerable rewards for individual investors by narrowing spreads and increasing liquidity. Most trades today can happen within fractions of a second, providing good prices and counterparties for those seeking to buy equities around the world.

But, at the same time, we have seen increased volatility and periodic dislocation. I think we all remember the flash crash a while back, but perhaps what did not get as much attention is that this—that was not the only incident. Just last month, on May 13, we had a series of mini flash crashes in a series of individual stocks. Such events do little to engender confidence and, indeed, may hinder investment in the stock market, adversely affecting the broader economy, particularly as it affects small cap stocks.

Gains in liquidity, I know, for most folks on the street are seen as the holy grail, but we have to ask ourselves at some point, at

(1)

what price this increased liquidity, and does sometimes simply progress and technological innovation bear other costs that need to be examined?

Some critics of current U.S. market structure place the blame on high frequency trading. For purposes of today's hearing, we are going to define high frequency trading to include computerized algorithmic trading of a number of varieties to essentially address when a computer is making a decision based on a program as opposed to a human.

In recent months, I know there has been a lot of renewed attention on this subject given to the publication of Michael Lewis's book, *Flash Boys*. And, I know many of my colleagues and I have growing concerns with what is happening in our markets that is leading to this erosion of confidence.

There are a few reforms that I would like to see the SEC implement to help strengthen confidence in the economy. First, and I think Senator Johanns will speak to this, as well, conducting a tick size pilot. As a former venture capitalist, I have concerns over front-running that impairs the ability of small companies to find adequate liquidity for their shares in the marketplace. This activity can adversely affect underwriting decisions or even the choice to go public, which obviously harms capital formation in its beginning.

Chairman White recently announced that the Commission is trying to finalize details of a potential pilot. I believe it should be for an adequate length of time, preferably more than a year, to capture enough data. It should also cover all of the trading venues, lit and dark, to ensure collection of accurate data.

Second, the SEC must expedite the implementation of a consolidated audit trail. Way back in May of 2010, a day after the infamous flash crash, then-Senator Ted Kaufman took to the floor. He talked about that challenge, and he and I both went to then-Senator Chris Dodd, who was Chair of this Committee, to require the SEC to report to Congress on the need for a consolidated audit trail, better order screening, and the risk posed by high frequency trading.

Unfortunately, more than 4 years later, we have seen little progress on our request, especially on the issue of the consolidated audit trail. The SEC has issued two extensions to the SROs and FINRA, delaying a proposal until September 30 of this year at the earliest. However, having this in place will help regulators decipher what is happening in the market, so we need to implement this ASAP, and I hope the SEC is listening.

Chairman White recently posed some reforms to enhance transparency in the market, and I thank her for moving on that, and it is clear that the SEC and the CFDC have a monumental task in policing our markets and they need full funding. I will continue to advocate for that as long as I am in this position.

Again, I look forward to hearing from our witnesses. I am going to move to Senator Johanns for his statement, and then, with the willingness of my colleagues, go ahead and introduce the panel and get to the testimony.

Senator Johanns.

STATEMENT OF SENATOR MIKE JOHANNS

Senator JOHANNS. Mr. Chairman, let me start out and say to the witnesses, thanks for being here. We appreciate it. I look forward to this hearing.

I also want to thank the Chairman for holding this hearing on high frequency trading. No doubt about it, it is getting attention these days, if not a lot of noise.

One thing that I probably need to be reminded about, as I think about my last months in the U.S. Senate, is if I have the capacity to write a book and get on ''60 Minutes'', I will probably get a lot of Congressional attention and I will be back here, sitting where you are sitting.

[Laughter.]

Senator JOHANNS. Maybe I can even convince Mr. Lewis to write a book about the need for housing finance reform or the overreach of EPA regulations. Both of those need attention.

Now, the spotlight is shining brighter. We all acknowledge that. The issue of high frequency trading, though, is not a new concept.

So, as I said, I look forward to the witnesses talking about the impact of high frequency trading on our economy, asking and answering questions, does the practice help or does it hurt investors?

Now, it does seem to me that retail investors really have never had it better. Costs are low. There seems to be ample competition. Market access is very easy these days. I definitely do not think the markets are rigged, as some have suggested.

However, I also believe that we cannot simply ignore certain market structure issues. We should always be encouraging liquidity. After all, why have a market if liquidity is not a part of it? We should be encouraging fairness. We should be encouraging transparency in the marketplace. We need to ensure that the U.S. remains the envy of the world when it comes to capital markets. I would just put out there, I do not think anyone does it better.

I also want to associate myself with comments made by Chairman Mary Jo White, who I have a lot of confidence in. She recently, in a public speech, said this, and I am quoting, ''We should not roll back the technology clock or prohibit algorithmic trading, but should assess the extent to which computer-driven trading may be working against investors rather than for them.'' There is a lot said in that quote.

America has always encouraged innovation. We want fastest. We want strongest. We want most powerful. I can relate to this. Growing up on a dairy farm in Northern Iowa in the 1950s and then becoming Secretary of Agriculture, I have seen a lot of change in that arena. The equipment and technology now is so much faster. It is so much smarter. The combines are so far advanced over what we were doing. It is unbelievable, what has happened in that arena. Who benefits from that? The consumer benefits from that, because they have a supply of food that is just unparalleled in the world and pay less of their disposable income. Technology is a good thing. Our financial trading systems have, obviously, gone through a remarkable, if not similar, evolution.

I think everyone here today is concerned with investor confidence. So, from the witnesses today, I would like to hear how small investors and small companies are affected in today's trading world. How do they fare?

As I said earlier, it seems that technology developments over the last several years have benefited retail investors by making the equity markets more accessible and affordable for the moms and the pops in Nebraska. But, investors are also, understandably, concerned when news stories suggest that the deck is somehow stacked, that the stock market has become an insider's game, that it cannot be trusted. So, I hope that we can talk about these real or perceived problems today.

Also, I am concerned with investor confidence in the small cap company space. The goal for every stock is liquidity. Can you market that stock? While the market seems to work fine for a large, if not blue chip, stock, the smaller public companies have not fared as well.

I know there has been discussion about widening tick sizes for smaller emerging growth companies. There was legislation on the House side that directs the SEC to issue a pilot program to test whether wider trading increments will promote more active trading and boost liquidity for smaller companies. Interestingly enough, this House bill passed 412 to four. I do believe that is part of what spurred the SEC to act. A House vote of 412 to four on a complex piece of legislation is almost unheard of, a remarkable result.

So, I would like to get the panel's thoughts on the pilot program and also hear about any other special market structure reform ideas that will benefit the small investor, the Main Street companies, those folks who are trying to find their place in this market.

Mr. Chairman, a great hearing today. I compliment you for calling it. Some very, very important issues that can have significant economic consequences to our States and to our country. Thank you very much.

Chairman WARNER. Thank you, Senator Johanns.

We have been joined by Senator Reed, who was longtime Chair of this Subcommittee, and Senator Warren, who brings, obviously, a wealth of knowledge to this subject. And, with their discretion, I am going to go ahead and introduce the witnesses and we can get started.

First, Mr. Hal Scott is the Nomura Professor at Harvard Law School, where he has taught since 1975, and Director ofthe Committee on Capital Markets Regulation. Professor Scott teaches courses on capital market regulation, international finance and securities regulation. He is currently Director of Lazard and a member of the Bretton Woods Committee and a past Governor of the American Stock Exchange. It is my understanding, as well, is he taught Senator Reed——

Senator REED. He did, without any effect.

[Laughter.]

Chairman WARNER. ——and has worked with, obviously, a colleague of Senator Warren's. When I was there, I did not have a chance to take one of his courses, but I look forward to his testimony.

Mr. Jeffrey Solomon is Chief Executive Officer of Cowen and Company and a Director of the Cowen Group. Mr. Solomon is responsible for overseeing all of Cowen and Company's business, including investment banking, capital market sales, and trading and research. Mr. Solomon is also a member of the Committee on Capital Markets Regulation as well as the Cochair of the Equity Capital Formation Task Force, a group of professionals from across America's start-up and small cap company ecosystems. Thank you and welcome, Mr. Solomon.

And, Mr. Andrew Brooks is Vice President of T. Rowe Price, where he is head of U.S. Equity Trading. He joined the firm in 1980 as an equity trader and assumed his current role in 1992. Mr. Brooks is currently a member of the Investment Company Institute Equity Markets Advisory Committee—that is a mouthful—and is on the board of the National Organization of Investment Professionals. Welcome, Mr. Brooks.

So, we will get to the testimony. Professor Scott.

STATEMENT OF HAL S. SCOTT, NOMURA PROFESSOR AND DIRECTOR, PROGRAM ON INTERNATIONAL FINANCIAL SYSTEMS, HARVARD LAW SCHOOL

Mr. SCOTT. Thank you, Chairman Warner, Ranking Member Johanns, and Members of the Subcommittee, for permitting me to testify before you today on the impact of high frequency trading on investor confidence and capital formation in U.S. equity markets. I am testifying in my own capacity and do not purport to represent the view of any organizations with which I am affiliated.

High frequency trading, or HFT, is a topic that has generated significant attention in recent years, intensifying more recently with the publication of Michael Lewis's book, *Flash Boys*. It is my intention to provide a thoughtful response to a debate that has sometimes been fraught with frenzied emotion.

Let me be clear at the outset. The emergence of high frequency trading activity in and of itself has not negatively affected our secondary markets. Our secondary markets remain strong, with roughly 50 percent of global exchange trading occurring on U.S. exchanges. With roughly half of this volume generated by HFT firms, the increased liquidity provided by HFTs lead to decreased costs of stock issuance, thus improving capital formation. And, of course, improved capital formation for our businesses leads to higher growth in the real economy.

Transaction costs for retail and institutional investors have also been in continual decline over the past 10 years, as evidenced by current bid-ask spreads, and have fallen by 50 percent since 2006 and brokerage commissions that are at historic lows. Retail investors can now trade for less than $10 a trade.

Since many retail investors access the equity markets indirectly through institutional funds or advisors, like mutual funds, institutional costs are highly relevant to retail investors, as well. Leading financial economists find that the average transaction costs for institutional orders are also at an all-time low.

Investor confidence in our markets also remains strong. Since the 2010 Flash Crash, there has been a net inflow of more than $50 billion in holdings of U.S.-listed companies and a total net inflow of nearly $500 billion in all exchange-traded products. Clearly, investors are not fleeing from our equity markets due to perceived threats of high frequency trading.

Moreover, experts have found that high frequency trading has not caused an increase in stock market volatility, although I think we will go around a little bit on that. And, the SEC has also largely addressed future Flash Crash concerns by implementing single stock circuit breakers and revising marketwide circuit breakers that will temporarily halt trading if price movements become too volatile.

Critics of HFT have questioned the fairness of allowing certain traders to benefit from their physical proximity to an exchange, known as colocation, and have access to faster data feeds. However, the SEC requires exchanges to offer such access to all market participants at the same cost, and remember, a large number of retail investors trade through these institutions who have such access. Over 90 percent of market participants have access to such services, including retail investors indirectly.

Thus, it is hard to argue that the U.S. equity market is broken as a result of the emergence of high frequency trading. Nonetheless, there is always room for targeted improvement of the current regulatory structure, and I would now like to present a few specific proposals.

First, regulators should consider mandating and harmonizing exchange-level so-called kill switched. A kill switch is a mechanism that would halt a particular firm's trading activity when a preestablished exposure threshold has been breached, thus stopping erroneous orders and preventing any further uncontrolled accumulation of positions. This would act against a single firm.

Second, they might consider addressing the volume of order message traffic generally, which can create market instability, by establishing order-to-trade ratios, and regulators should consider charging fees for extreme message traffic in particular circumstances.

Third, regulators should consider abolishing immunity that exchanges have from liabilities for losses from market disruptions based on their SRO status, which might better align the exchanges' incentives to limit potentially risky trading that could pose widespread operational risk.

And, I also endorse the idea, and I think it is quite important, of a much better audit trail, the CAT effort that the SEC is underway with, and I agree with Senator Warner that they should act sooner rather than later on that, because knowing what happens is the key to all of our understanding, and that audit trail will help give us knowledge that we currently do not have about how trading is actually being conducted.

In concluding my remarks, I wish to reiterate that the strength of U.S. equity markets has positively affected capital formation, and by extension, promoted job creation. Any changes in HFT regulation should be based on a factually careful assessment of abuses and regulation to fix them without harming the overall performance of our markets.

Thank you, and I look forward to your questions.

Chairman WARNER. Thank you, Professor Scott.

Mr. Solomon.

STATEMENT OF JEFFREY M. SOLOMON, CHIEF EXECUTIVE OFFICER, COWEN AND COMPANY, LLC, AND COCHAIR, EQUITY CAPITAL FORMATION TASK FORCE

Mr. SOLOMON. Good morning, Chairman Warner, Ranking Member Johanns, and the Members of the Subcommittee. Thank you for inviting me to speak today regarding high frequency trading's impact on the economy.

My name is Jeffrey Solomon and I am the Chief Executive Officer at Cowen and Company, an emerging growth investment bank focused on servicing growth-oriented companies in key sectors of our economy. Along with Scott Cooper, the Chief Operating Officer of Andreessen Horowitz, I am also the Cochair of the Equity Capital Formation Task Force. And, interestingly, I have spent most of my career as an institutional investor in equities, so I understand this issue from many sides.

Over the past year, there has been significant debate about the economic impact of HFT, high frequency trading, on the equity capital markets in the United States and how the rise in their trading activity has introduced increased market risk and volatility. We would argue that the debate surrounding HFT is actually symptomatic of a more complex market structure that encourages potentially counterproductive trading behavior, behavior that limits true market depth and trading volume in many stocks and hinders investors' ability to buy and sell those stocks in small cap companies, in particular.

This has resulted in reduced availability of capital for small public companies to expand their businesses and create valuable private sector jobs. As such, any debate about the pros and cons of HFT really needs to address the structure of the equity market that has given rise to its existence.

The rise in electronic trading and the regulations that followed resulted in new market structure for equities that was intended to benefit investors, and today, our market's structure is marked by speed of execution, lower transaction costs, and sub-penny increments, a dynamic which works well enough in highly liquid large cap stocks, but fosters opacity and liquidity in small cap stocks. For investors in small cap stocks, true price discovery is far more important than speed of execution.

As a result, it has become more costly and difficult for institutional investors, who are the primary providers of growth capital to emerging companies, to invest, trade, and make markets in small caps. Companies with market caps of $750 million and below represent only 2 percent of the daily trading volume in the United States, and, on average, are only 30 percent held by institutions. Without meaningful institutional ownership, capital formation for small companies has declined to levels well below historic levels and has impeded price appreciation for many individual investors, as well.

While the JOBS Act had made it easier for emerging growth companies to go public—the number of IPOs has increased since its passage—little has been done to improve the quality of secondary market trading in small stocks. And, to address these concerns, the Equity Capital Formation Task Force presented its findings and recommendations to the United States Treasury in a report which sets out two areas for consideration.

One is to encourage increased liquidity in small cap stocks by fostering a simpler, more orderly market structure for small cap stocks, and to expand capital for small cap and micro cap companies by completing regulatory changes outlined in the JOBS Act in accordance with Reg A Plus. These recommendations are designed to enhance capital formation for small companies while balancing the needs of investor protection and preserving many of the important improvements made to market structure that investors have enjoyed since the advent of decimalization.

In order to improve market structure, we have recommended that the SEC implement a well designed pilot program that allows for a true empirical test on the effects of both wider spreads and limited trading increments in small caps, which we believe will encourage fundamental buyers and sellers to meaningfully engage with each other. By designing a pilot that requires all market participants to cluster their bids and offers at fewer discrete increments, and by limiting the ability of certain market participants to, quote-unquote, ''price improve'' in sub-penny increments, we will be able to observe whether or not the volume and depth necessary to enhance liquidity in small caps will improve. Improved trading liquidity begets cheaper and more efficient access to capital for these companies, and improved access to capital translates into increased job creation in the private sector.

One of the most important aspects of designing a successful pilot program is ensuring that such a pilot program is allowed to operate for a long enough period for time to gather meaningful data around whether or not the changes to the market structure are having desired effects. We strongly believe that market participants, especially those that use algorithms and trade frequently, will need time to adjust their trading practices and/or business models in order to adopt to the new market structure. However, just as they adopted to decimalization and other market structure changes over the past 15 years, we are confident that they will adapt to these proposed market changes in the small cap market, as well.

It appears as if the SEC, under the leadership of Chairwoman White, has made a strong commitment to enhancing overall liquidity of the capital markets in general and for small companies, more importantly. The Task Force supports the data-driven results oriented approach that the Commission has espoused publicly over the last 9 months. Our members continue to advocate that a one-size-fits-all market structure does not meet the needs of any market participants.

We praise Congress on the passage of the JOBS Act, which demonstrated that a well-drafted legislation and regulation can meet the dual needs of fostering increased formation for capital while maintaining investor protection. Now is the time to create momentum, or to capitalize on the momentum created by the JOBS Act to take additional steps to further the growth of America's most promising private and public growth companies. We owe it to those Americans seeking jobs and those companies creating those jobs to try and adjust a small part of the market structure in order to improve access to capital.

I thank you for this time and I welcome your questions and dialogue.

Chairman WARNER. Thank you, Mr. Solomon.

Mr. Brooks.

STATEMENT OF ANDREW M. BROOKS, VICE PRESIDENT AND HEAD OF U.S. EQUITY TRADING, T. ROWE PRICE ASSOCIATES, INC.

Mr. BROOKS. Good morning. Chairman Warner, Ranking Member Johanns, and distinguished Members of the Senate Subcommittee on Securities, Insurance, and Investment, thank you for the opportunity to testify today on behalf of T. Rowe Price regarding the impact of high frequency trading on the economy.

My name is Andy Brooks. I am a Vice President and Head of U.S. Equity Trading at T. Rowe Price. This is my 34th year on the trading desk at T. Rowe Price. T. Rowe Price was founded in 1937 and is a Baltimore-based advisor, serving more than 10 million individual and institutional investor accounts.

Since I last testified before this Committee in September of 2012, we have seen considerable turnover in Congress, this Committee, and at the U.S. Securities and Exchange Commission. However, there has been little change in addressing the issues discussed 21 months ago, although we do applaud the SEC's efforts in implementing limit up, limit down controls and developing the consolidated audit trail. Additionally, we are encouraged by Chair Mary Jo White's recent comments suggesting a heightened focus on improving market structure. And, we appreciate this Committee's continued interest in improving our markets.

However, order routing practices, payment for order flow, maker/taker pricing, market data arbitrage, and the myopic quest for speed are all issues that remain unaddressed. In addition, we have grown increasingly concerned about the growth of dark pools and the challenges of the direct fast feed operating alongside the slow security information processor feed.

Although this hearing is focused on HFT, we believe HFT is merely symptomatic of larger market structure problems. We are cautious not to lump all electronic trading into the class of HFT, and, further, we do not believe that all HFT is detrimental to the market. We are supportive of genuine market making. However, we acknowledge there are predatory strategies in the marketplace that have been enabled by our overly complex and fragmented trading markets. Those parties utilizing such strategies are exploiting market structure issues to their benefit and to the overall market's and individual investors' detriment.

We question whether the functional roles of an exchange and a broker-dealer have become blurred over the years, creating inherent conflicts of interest that may warrant regulatory action. It seems clear that since the exchanges have migrated to for-profit models, a conflict has arisen between the pursuit of volume and resulting revenue and the obligation to assure an orderly marketplace for all investors. The fact that 11 exchanges and over 50 dark pools operate on a given day seems to create a model that is susceptible to manipulative practices.

If a market participant's sole function is to interposition themselves between buyers and sellers, we question the value of such a role and believe it puts an unneeded strain on the system. It begs the question as to whether investors were better served when the exchanges functioned more akin to a public utility. Should exchanges with de minimis market share enjoy the regulatory protection that is offered by their status as exchanges or should they be ignored?

Additionally, innovations in technology and competition, including HFT, have increased market complexity and fragmentation and have diluted an investor's ability to gauge best execution. For example, in the race to increase market share, exchanges in alternative trading venues continue to offer various order types to compete for investor order flow. Many of these types facilitate strategies that can benefit certain market participants at the expense of long-term investors, and while seemingly appropriate, often, such order types are used in connection with predatory trading strategies. We are supportive of incremental efforts, such as recent initiatives by the New York Stock Exchange to eliminate 12 order types from their offerings.

We also believe that increased intraday volatility over the past year is just symptomatic of an overly complex market. Though commission rates and spreads have been reduced, volatility continues to be alarmingly high. It was refreshing to see a recent report from RBC Capital Markets examining the impact of intraday volatility and exposing the high cost to investors. Most academics only look at close to close market volatility.

Increased market complexity results in a lack of investor confidence. A recent Gallup Poll noted that American household ownership of stocks continues to trend well below historic norms. One can never be sure what drives investor behavior, but it seems clear to us that we need to do a better job of earning investors' confidence in our markets. Those investors who have stayed on the sidelines in recent years, for whatever reason, have missed out on significant equity returns. We worry that the erosion of investor confidence can undermine our capital markets, which are so important to the economy, job growth, and global competitiveness.

Over the past two decades, the markets have benefited from innovations in technology and competition. Generally, markets open at 9:30, they close at 4, and trades settle efficiently and seamlessly.

Vibrant and robust markets function best when there are varied investment opinions, styles, and approaches. However, given the myriad of ways to engage in the markets, we feel that investors would benefit from an increased focus on market structure, particularly features that enable predatory and manipulative practices. Disruptive HFT strategies are akin to a tax loophole that has been exploited and needs to be closed. Market participants utilizing such strategies are essentially making a riskless bet on the market, like a gambler who places a bet on a race that has already been won and for which he knows the outcome.

In the spirit of advancing the interests of all investors, we might make the following suggestions. We envision a pilot program where all payments for order flow, maker/taker fees, and other inducements for order flow routing are eliminated. We also envision a pilot that incorporates wider minimum spreads and some version of a "trade at" rule, which we believe would lead to genuine price improvement. These programs should include a spectrum of stocks across market caps, average trading volumes, among other factors.

Additionally, we would advocate for a pilot program that would mandate minimum trade sizes for dark pools. Dark pools were originally constructed to encourage larger trading interests, and it seems perverse that many venues on the lit markets, or exchanges, have a larger average trade size than dark pools.

HFT and market structure issues were recently brought into the public spotlight by Michael Lewis and his book, *Flash Boys.* Sometimes, it takes a storyteller like Mr. Lewis to bring attention needed to an issue, and we hope that all parties involved will come together and seize this opportunity to improve our markets. Again, we would advocate for pilot programs to test and ultimately implement measured, yet significant, changes.

On behalf of T. Rowe Price, our clients, and shareholders, I want to thank the Committee for this opportunity to share our views on how we can together make our markets as good as they can be.

Chairman WARNER. Thank you, gentlemen. Very good testimony.

I am going to ask you to put 5 minutes on the clock for each of us. I will try to be brief. I would ask you to be fairly brief in your responses, so I am going to try to get as many questions as I can in my time.

I have a particular bias, as a former venture capitalist, on the notion of small cap stocks, and would point out to my colleagues that data by the Kauffman Foundation has pointed out that literally, I think, 80 percent of all net new jobs that have been created in the last 30 years in America have come from startup enterprises. So, how we accelerate that is, I think, a policy focus that we would all share.

Professor Scott and Mr. Brooks, do you share Mr. Solomon's belief that there should be some level of differentiation between small cap and larger caps and pilots like the tick size pilot moving forward? Other suggestions? Professor Scott.

Mr. SCOTT. Well, I am a member of Jeff's Task Force and I do agree with——

Chairman WARNER. Press your microphone button.

Mr. SCOTT. I am a member of Jeff's Task Force and endorse the recommendations for a pilot study on increasing the tick size for small caps. I think the result will be to show that with more trading and more liquidity, you know, we will encourage small caps. But, I think it is important to do a pilot study. There is a lot of controversy around this question as to whether increasing the tick size will really increase trading and we need to find out. So, I am certainly in favor of the pilot program.

Chairman WARNER. Do you believe that the basic premise that HFTs potentially could disadvantage small cap stocks at this point? Do you think—I guess, obviously, you are on that Committee, but I took that as——

Mr. SCOTT. I am not sure I see a connection between HFT per se and disadvantaging small caps. I think what we need to do is increase the tick size and see what results, even with high frequency traders as they might adjust to trading in such an environment. Maybe they will trade less, OK, with a bigger tick differential. But, that will be their adjustment to an increased tick size.

Chairman WARNER. Mr. Brooks, and then we will let Mr. Solomon have a——

Mr. BROOKS. Senator, my sense is that this pilot program is way overdue. We have been talking about it for a long time. I think there is vigorous debate about whether—what will happen as an outcome, and I think it is time to try. You know, we are very interested in increasing displayed liquidity, especially in small cap stocks, and I think a larger tick size, the cost—the barrier to entry for someone who is trying to interposition themselves there will grow and perhaps they will be discouraged from playing in that sandbox. Greater displayed liquidity, I think, would be good for investors and would attract, perhaps, more interest, investor interest in those names.

You know, at the heart of the issue is trying to figure out a mechanism to allow someone to tell the story of small companies, to promote small stocks, promote in a good way, to tell the story about the growth and the potential. We have removed so many incentives for brokers and others, financial advisors, to tell the story of a stock that it has made it hard for people to figure out why they should care about small companies.

Mr. SOLOMON. Listen, we have written extensively about it and I totally agree. I think one thing, to augment what Professor Scott said, is it is not just wider spreads. It is wider spreads and limited trading increments, and this is really important. There are a lot of small cap stocks that trade at wider than a penny. What we have talked about here is having a minimum bid and offer.

So, when a stock trades wide and all of a sudden there is interest or displayed liquidity, all of a sudden, it rushes to a penny, and that precludes institutional investors like Andy, who make up a significant portion of the net worth of American households invested in stocks. They cannot get access to the small companies that exhibit the best growth, because by the time he shows up to buy a meaningful stake, it is reduced to a penny and they are just waiting for him to sit there and indicate size so they can pick him off.

And, so, what we have said is, if you forced people to cluster at bids and offers, fewer of them, at five-cent increments, there are only 20 places where you can cluster in between each dollar. And, you limit the trading at the bid, at the offer, or one price in the middle. That should be ample for any fundamental buyer and seller to do price discovery and it limits this game or casino type behavior we have seen with sub-penny price improvement.

Chairman WARNER. Let me get one last question in, and I am going to take as a quick nod, yes, that we ought to move forward and keep the pressure on the SEC to move on their consolidated audit trail efforts.

Mr. SOLOMON. Yes.

Mr. BROOKS. Yes.

Chairman WARNER. Let me try to get Mr. Solomon and Professor Scott's comments. Mr. Brooks has got a fairly aggressive outline of reforms, including, for example, the pilot of getting rid of some of the, what appears to be inherent conflicts on the maker/taker circumstances that we all discussed. You have got some general agreement. Would each of you go as far as Mr. Brooks has gone, Professor Scott and then Mr. Solomon.

Mr. SOLOMON. Go ahead. You are up.

Mr. SCOTT. He wants to defer to me. I am not—I do not think so. I am not ready for pilot studies yet on these issues. I think the first step is that we should get the SEC study done and see what they come up with on these issues, and we should hope that they act expeditiously. I might say in their defense that they have had a lot on their plate for the last several years and they have gotten around a market structure now and I think they are going full bore on it. So, I think we need to get a lot more information about the problems, focus in on what the abuses are.

I also think we have to be careful about pilot studies. While I endorse Jeff's pilot study, we can confuse the market a lot with a lot of pilot studies going on at the same time, where different stocks trade in different ways. And, so, we have to be very careful, it seems to me, about—and, then, when you design a pilot study, you have to have a control. So, some people are not going to be trading under the pilot. Other people will. We do not know exactly how the SEC will devise their pilot, but if you do not have that, then you do not have a controlled experiment. So, it—and it all depends on how you design this pilot, OK.

So, I am not ready for pilots on this issue. I think on tick size, we have had a lot of discussion over several years. A lot of work has been done on it. SEC has studied it intensively, and I think we are ready for a pilot. I do not think we are ready for pilots on these other issues.

Mr. SOLOMON. So, I think we designed our proposals here to engage in—within the context of the existing maker/taker regime. So, we have said that this only is 2 percent of the daily average trading volume, so the people that are making a fair amount of money trading large volumes should not be impacted by a small cap stock because it is not a significant portion of their revenue.

On the issue of maker/taker, it is not—if you were setting up a market structure from scratch, I think we can acknowledge that it is not the most ideal economic way to incent behavior. But, it is what it is, in part because we got here through regulation. And, if we are going to undo maker/taker, we had better have a pretty good idea of how we are going to incent buyers and sellers to meet and how that is going to occur before we pull that plug or we will see a material drop in liquidity, simply because people will have to adjust their business models.

Chairman WARNER. I would simply say, I concur with Professor Scott, the SEC has got a lot on their plate, one of the reasons why I support full funding, but we also have to see the kind of—we need to see the action from them.

Senator Johanns.

Senator JOHANNS. Thank you, Mr. Chairman.

Every one of you presented fascinating testimony, interesting testimony, and I think it raised so many complicated issues. So, let me, if I might, take a step back here and ask you about your preference in terms of how we approach this, because if we just spent the next hour writing down the significant issues, I will bet you we

14

could not get it done in that hour. And, I am trying to figure out process-wise what is the best approach here, because the one thing we do not want to do is mess up a system that has done some awfully good things. Now, there may be some issues, and I do not want to necessarily debate that.

Process-wise—Professor, I will start with you—would it be your preference that we look to the Chairman of the SEC, the SEC itself, to start working through these issues, identify approaches, and use its regulatory powers to deal with these issues, or would you rather have Congress try to—you know how we are functioning these days—would you rather have Congress grab a hold of this issue and see what we can do here? And, we have broad shoulders. You can tell us what you think and we will not be offended, I promise you.

Mr. SCOTT. Senator, I have dealt with a lot of complexity in my life. This is one of the most complex areas you will ever encounter. When you go through particular questions of this trade or that trade and who is getting an advantage and how it works, it is very complicated.

Senator JOHANNS. Yes.

Mr. SCOTT. And, I think that says caution to legislation before we have the experts, OK, do their best job to formulate what the problems are and what the solutions are. And, I think your role for the time being is to make sure that the SEC goes forward on this. And, by the way, I am one that thinks the SEC should be adequately funded to do these kinds of jobs. I think it is totally unfair to the SEC to put a lot on their plate and not give them the money to do it.

Senator JOHANNS. OK.

Mr. SCOTT. So, I think, you know, let us have the SEC do it. You keep the pressure on for them to do it and you review their findings.

Senator JOHANNS. Mr. Solomon.

Mr. SOLOMON. I think it is a very complex issue, but I think there is actually a relatively few number of changes you can make, and I think, well within an hour, you could have it laid out. It is actually pretty straightforward if you start with some basic premise, which is simpler—simpler markets. Simpler markets foster better behavior from fundamental buyers and sellers. We have just got a market structure that basically has gotten away from, do you want to own this at this price? Do you want to sell this at this price? And——

Senator JOHANNS. But, let me ask you about that. You talked about sub-penny price improvement. Tell me, just as straightforward as you can, does Mr. Brooks win with that?

Mr. SOLOMON. No.

Senator JOHANNS. Who is the winner and who is the loser when you do that?

Mr. SOLOMON. So, sub-penny price improvement is what enables electronic market makers to aggregate retail order flow and give them the execution inside the national best bid and offer. So, if the regime requires you to give a retail order or individual order an execution at the best bid and offer when it hits the floor, or when it actually gets displayed, the best way to ensure you do that is to crawl inside whatever bid and offer there is by a tenth of a penny.

Andy and his compatriots on the institutional side do not benefit from that because they are not individual orders. So, his ability to get an——he can stand there at the bid, and sit or stand there on the offer, and a lot of shares can trade at the bid and the offer and he does not get a fill. That is a problem, because a lot of folks, or a lot of other intermediaries are aggregating positions or selling positions in the hopes of being able to sell to him at a price higher or buy it from him at a price lower——

Senator JOHANNS. And——

Mr. SOLOMON. ——and that is what is happening with sub——that is where sub-pennying becomes a very difficult market issue.

Senator JOHANNS. Right. As an individual investor, then, do I benefit?

Mr. SOLOMON. So, you benefit in a couple of ways. So, you certainly benefit by having five-dollar commissions. This is the maker/taker regime is what underpins cheap execution.

Senator JOHANNS. Yes.

Mr. SOLOMON. We question whether or not you actually benefit, because if you buy individual——most individuals are owning stocks that are in the growth range. We have seen what the disparity is in terms of individual ownership. Seventy percent——if you go to sub-$250 million companies, it is, like, 85 percent owned by individuals. The only reason to own those stocks is because you think they are going to go higher and because——and, what makes them go higher? Institutional involvement. So, there is——now, the market is biased against getting people like Andy involved in small cap stocks. So, while you may have gotten a five-dollar execution, did you——and, you may have actually given up the opportunity for price improvement.

Senator JOHANNS. But, I may want the five-dollar execution.

Mr. SOLOMON. Mm-hmm.

Senator JOHANNS. You know, I remember the good old days when this did not exist and I had a few stocks and I called a broker and they charged me an arm and a leg and said, ''I will settle up with you in 7 days,'' and I am kind of going, wait a second. I think I lost on that deal.

Mr. SOLOMON. So, there is a middle ground.

Senator JOHANNS. And, the fact that you are telling me, ''But, Mike, your stock might have gone up,'' is not very reassuring to me. I want a five-dollar trade. What is wrong with that?

Mr. SOLOMON. There is nothing wrong with wanting five-dollar trades, and we think there is enough competition in the marketplace that people will compete on commission. Listen, we should not be competing on commissions as a way to drive revenues. We should be competing on investment ideas. So, go to your broker that gives you——that shows you over a period of time that they can consistently make you money. Then commission dollars actually do not matter that much, and we——but we should not have——

Senator JOHANNS. What if I am a rugged individualist, and quite honestly, I do not want to deal with a broker.

Mr. SOLOMON. OK.

Senator JOHANNS. I want to go someplace. I want to pay my five dollars for a trade. I want to give—I want to get access to all of the information they can give me. I want to dig into it. I want to study it. And, I am not alone. And, I am using me as a hypothetical here because I do not buy and sell or trade. I do not trade stocks. But, having said that, millions of Americans have warmed up to this idea and they like it.

Mr. SOLOMON. Which is fine. There will still be people that offer cheap execution because we have got a lot of benefits. So, I think it is fine. There will still be cheap execution.

What is missing in this, though, is a little bit of balance, because Andy manages a bunch of money in your 401(k) or in your pension, I mean, all these other areas, all these other ways that you access the market, and he is being precluded from participating in growth in a vital part of the American economy because the current market structure is overly focused on cheap execution or cheap commissions.

And, I think there is a balance here, which is why we have said there is a different regime, potentially, that could go on for the smaller companies. There is not a one-size-fits-all answer here. Five-dollar executions are great. I use them. I love them. But, you do not have to give that up and still foster capital formation and encourage price discovery.

Senator JOHANNS. I have exhausted my time, but I do have one question. What percentage of trades on a given day or a given month would be the five-dollar execution versus the Andys of the world?

Mr. SOLOMON. I do not think I have that information. I think one of the challenges that the exchanges and the SEC is determining is what actually constitutes a retail order flow.

Senator JOHANNS. OK.

Mr. SOLOMON. That is a hotly debated discussion point, because there is—I think people feel like if we are really, truly protecting individual investors, everybody is on board with that. But, there are people who masquerade around as individual investors who are really high frequency or professional traders who are accessing their five-dollar trading accounts, and that does not quite seem like it is right. And so it is very difficult, actually, to know. I cannot tell—and, by the way, everything trades in hundred lots today, so it is really hard to be able to discern between an institutional order and a retail order. There is no real way to capture that data, to the best of my knowledge.

Senator JOHANNS. Thank you, Mr. Chairman.

Chairman WARNER. I think you raised a good point, Senator Johanns. The question I would have, and I am going to let Senator Warren get an extra couple minutes, is just that would that rugged individualist who gets the five-dollar trade be offended if somebody in that tiny spread is making perhaps inappropriate profits because you have got the incentives misaligned? But, I imagine maybe Senator Warren might go down that direction.

Senator Warren.

Senator WARREN. So, thank you, Mr. Chairman, and thank you all for being here.

And, I do. I want to pick up on that line. The question for me is not so much about the cost savings from all electronic trading, it is the question about the so-called high frequency traders. And, for me, the term ''high frequency trading'' seems wrong. You know, this is not trading. Traders have good days and bad days. Some days, they make good trades and they make lots of money, and some days, they have bad trades and they lose a lot of money.

But, high frequency traders have only good days. In its recent IPO filing, the high frequency trading firm Virtu reported that it had been trading for 1,238 days and it had made money on 1,237 of those days. Now, I do not know what happened on the one bad day, but I assume a computer somewhere got fired.

The question is that high frequency trading firms are not making money by taking on risks. They are making money by charging a very small fee to investors, and the question is whether they are charging that fee in return for providing a valuable service, or they are charging that fee by just skimming a little money off the top of every trade.

So, let me start there. Mr. Brooks, the defenders of high frequency trading often claim that they provide liquidity to the market. There is always someone willing to buy whatever it is that investor is selling. What is your view on that?

Mr. BROOKS. That is a great question, Senator. I think our view is that is a convenient answer by them. You know, the markets functioned pretty well prior to high frequency trading strategies being adopted. You know, if 95 out of 100 times that you have said you want to buy 100 shares of GE you canceled that trade, that expression of trading interest before anybody can get to you, I sort of question the true intent of what you are doing.

Now, I think it is important to be clear, some high frequency trading strategies are legitimate. They are market making. They are statistical arbitrage. They are buying stocks in a basket against an index or something like that. But, a lot of these strategies really, our understanding—and by the way, I agree with both Mr. Solomon and Professor Scott, this market subject is incredibly complex—but, so much of what a high frequency trading strategy might be is to act, to draw a reaction, and then to profit from your reaction. So, they flank you. They pivot around you. They really have no intention of trading. They just sort of want to see what you are going to do, and once they know what you are going to do, they can step in front of you.

Senator WARREN. Right. So, you would argue this is not adding liquidity to the marketplace——

Mr. BROOKS. We think there is a huge difference between liquidity and volume. They trump the liquidity side and we are, like, wow. Before you guys came along, we seemed to be fine, or seemed to be better, in some respects.

And, I do think it is important here to identify that retail investors declare victory. You are in great shape. The five-dollar trade, instant access, awesome. But, a big part of your portfolio, of your nest egg, might be invested with people like us. And, in that part of the market, it is not such a good trade because you have people that are taking advantage of your being in a market for a longer period of time. When you are buying 100 shares, you are there for

2 seconds and you are done. You declare victory. You go home. It is great.

But, let us say you have a million shares to buy. I might be there all day, and all day, those other interlopers, if you will, have an opportunity to step in front of, take advantage of, sniff out our order, all those kinds of things. And, that is troubling to the market. That is where we could be better.

Mr. SOLOMON. I also think, by the way, that there are—the liquidity providers are there when it is convenient for them to be there. So, I would ask the question, are they really providing liquidity, because I know if I am an individual investor and I want to sell and I am in a line with everybody else, they have no obligation to be there. In fact, arguably, when that starts to happen in the market, the thing that concerns me most is all a lot of these algorithms look and tradeoff the same trends. So, if we start to get one-sided in the market in the other direction, they will widen their bids and offers and then we no longer have a market that is—has a responsibility to provide liquidity, a buyer of last resort.

Senator WARREN. So, if I am following you, Mr. Solomon, you are saying that they are really adding volatility to the market, volume to the market, without adding true liquidity to the market.

Mr. SOLOMON. It can be true liquidity. It is just not true liquidity when you might actually need to get true liquidity, because there is no obligation. So, they will trade as long as there is liquidity, and we have seen in small caps, for example, when there is no activity, they do not trade until there is activity. Then, they trade. And, so, that is not really providing that liquidity. That is, like, moths to the flame. There is a flame. Let us fly there.

And, so, that is not real adding—it looks to the casual observer as if there is a lot of volume, but is there real fundamental buyers and sellers or is it just a bunch of people crawling in there when they think there are real buyers and sellers around and creating activity that really does not add to the ability for Andy to aggregate a position or sell a position when he actually needs to do it.

And, I worry about the stability of the marketplace because when there is going to be—there will be, it is a matter of when—when there is selling, I wonder who is going to be there to actually buy it, because in the old days, we may not have liked the New York Stock Exchange and the things that they did and the money they made, but they stood there and bought stocks in 1987, down big, but they bought them and the market opened the next day.

And here, I am a little bit concerned, particularly around the Flash Crash. What happened there? You do not really need to do a lot of studying. A lot of algorithms said, oh, my God, this is unusual. I am going to widen my bids and offers because I do not understand what is happening. And then everybody did it. And, so, we are no better today in that regard than we were in 2010.

And, I think, that is actually the challenge in market structure, as opposed to whether HFT is good or bad. It is the market structure we live in, and HFT, sometimes it helps, sometimes it does not, but we are not in a good place market structure-wise.

Senator WARREN. All right. So, thank you, and—good. Actually, if I can just answer it, because the other argument you often hear is one about speed, that it speeds up the transactions. Mr. Brooks.

Mr. BROOKS. So, our view on speed is, you know, if your request for speed is singularly focused, I think it is reckless. And, what we have been led to understand about market structure and the quest for speed is when you are interested in speed, you remove safeguards and you remove some of the infrastructure and the underpinnings of the market. And, so, fortunately, we put in—the SEC put in the limit up, limit down, and some marketwide circuit breakers and that has been great. But, both the Flash Crash and Knight Capital situation were maybe driven by speed, and if that is the case, that is not good for anybody.

As investors, it is rare—it is rare that speed is important to us. Our average holding period is, like, 3 years. Why do I really care what is going to happen in a nanosecond?——

Senator WARREN. Well, I was going to say——

Mr. BROOKS. I do not.

Senator WARREN. ——I take it the speed difference we are talking about is measured is milliseconds——

Mr. BROOKS. You cannot even blink——

Senator WARREN. ——not in 7 days.

Mr. BROOKS. It is milliseconds, is right.

Senator WARREN. Yes.

Mr. BROOKS. It is nanoseconds. And, that advantage, that speed advantage, if it destabilizes, it seems to us that that is wrong. That is not right, and we ought to push back on that. Our view is, we really ought to just slow down, not walk away from technology, but let us take a deep breath here and really look at what we have, and I appreciate Professor Scott's admonition about the complexity of the market. But, we have got to make some progress.

You know, my boss says to me, "I do not really care how fast you are moving toward the goal, but please move in the right direction, will you?" If I am not moving in the right direction, I am in trouble. We have not been moving in the right direction. Oh, my God, we have got Dodd-Frank, we have got Volcker, we have got blah, blah, blah, all these things out there. They are always there. There is always a reason why you cannot do it today.

You know, we used to have a fellow that worked for us who used to talk about the phrase, "Today is the hardest day to invest." There is always something that might preclude you from doing something. Today is the hardest day to go after difficult market problems, because, gee whiz, I have got something else I have got to worry about.

Can we just start to make some progress? Please. We do not have the answers. Pilot programs give you the opportunity to generate data. Let the academics run wild, try and figure it out. Move in very incremental, careful ways. It is right, you have to have a control. You have got to know what you are trying to study and measure for. But, we can do that, and I think we can do that in a constructive way.

Senator WARREN. Well, I want to say, thank you very much, Mr. Chairman, on this. You know, high frequency trading reminds me a little of the scam in office space. You know, you take just a little bit of money from every trade in the hope that no one will complain. But, taking a little bit of money from zillions of trades adds up to billions of dollars in profits for these high frequency traders, and billions of dollars in losses for our retirement funds and our mutual funds and everybody else in the marketplace. It also means a tilt in the playing field for those who do not have the information or do not have the access to the speed, or who are not big enough to play in this game.

So, I want to see the SEC, the State agencies push forward in their investigations, and I think we should continue to do the same.

Thank you, Mr. Chairman.

Chairman WARNER. Thank you, Senator.

We will actually get another—let us each take another question. I have got another question, if you want to take another quick shot at this.

I just—I was in the technology business for a long time. The last thing you want to appear, particularly sitting in a chairman's seat, is like a Luddite. But, I do kind of—do feel at times there may have been some—and I want Professor Scott to give a rebuttal to this a little bit—that technology for the sake of technology, when speed becomes so quintessentially important, when the opportunity to colocate becomes an advantage that clearly larger firms have over smaller, and the ability to get your—where you locate your exchange becomes such a—the real estate decision becomes such a critical question.

And, I know that, Professor Scott, you said that the volatility has not increased. I actually thought that the intraday—again, volatility has gone up 5x since 1996. I want you to kind of mention that.

And, I do, and I do not know if any of you cited this study, but the study that shows the millennials are investing in the market at a lower percentage than anyone else. Now, is that a question of just financial uncertainty or is there—you would think, from the generation that would be more technology competent, there would be more willingness to accept this, but there seems to be perhaps a wariness amongst young folks that perhaps the system is being gamed.

Comments? Thoughts?

Mr. SCOTT. I would like to say at the outset that when we talk about the market, we are talking about lots of different trading systems in that market. And, one of the stories of *Flash Boys* was the attempt to design a better market, IEX. So, there is maker/taker, there is taker/maker out there. So, part of what we have to think about when we look at this is what are people gravitating to? If you give them taker/maker, are they using that system, or do they find something else that is wrong with it? So, the market is not just one thing that is working in the same direction, a lot of different trading systems, a lot of different ways to trade.

All right. Now, let me address your question, Senator, on volatility. There are many ways to measure it, OK. You can do it intraday, in which it is going up. You can do it day to day, week to week. I would say long-term investors who are key to the capital formation of our country are less interested in the amount of intraday volatility, you know, except for those people who are out sitting there on E*TRADE just trying to make a profit in 1 day.

We are talking about long-term investors, and it seems to me that their horizon on volatility is shorter than intraday.

The second thing I would say on volatility is that the CBOE Volatility Index, so-called VIX, has fallen to its lowest levels since 2007. What they measure is the 30-day expected volatility of the S&P 500. So, there is still a different measure that shows very low volatility.

Whatever the volatility is, or is not, it remains to be seen what high frequency trading's impact is on that volatility, because volatility—and this comes back to a question you asked—is driven by a lot of factors, only part of which, and maybe even a small part of which, may be trading system. We have been, since 2008, in a state of high uncertainty as to the future of our economy, OK, and that in and of itself—OK, every day, oh, I think we are OK, no, we are not OK, we have got this data, we have got that data—that kind of environment, where you are not certain of where we are going, produces volatility. And, so, I think the question, is the volatility coming from high frequency trading or it is coming from something else.

On all of these issues, we need more understanding, more transparency, more information, OK, which is, hopefully, the SEC is going to provide.

Now, in terms of the millennials issue, so, you know, the question is, are younger people in this country increasingly sort of afraid to invest in the market? When those people were questioned, only 5 percent of them actually said that they had an aggressive risk tolerance. So, what these people are saying is that we are very conservative. We have a risk aversion. That 5 percent is a pretty low number. And, so, you have to then ask, well, why are they risk averse? Is it because there are high frequency traders operating out there? I do not think so. It is because of the nature of what we have seen in the market and great uncertainty about our economic future. And, I think, that is what is preventing people from investing.

Now, that being said, Japan has had a longstanding problem of not getting people into their markets, and I think some people might analyze the reason for that as that the people do not trust the fairness of that market. So, we should not neglect fairness as a possible explanation, but there are powerful economic fundamentals here, in my view, that have been driving volatility and been driving less investor confidence.

Chairman WARNER. Thank you. We will go to Senator Reed and then back to Senator Johanns.

Senator REED. Well, thank you very much, Mr. Chairman, and thank you, gentlemen, for your testimony. I apologize. I had to be down at the Defense Appropriations hearing with Secretary Hagel and the Chairman of the Joint Chiefs of Staff.

But, Mr. Brooks, in 2012, you were here before and testifying and——

Mr. BROOKS. Nice to see you again, Senator.

Senator REED. Yes, sir, and it'sgood to see Professor Scott. As I said, previously, he led me to great intellectual waters, but I did not understand how to drink, so thank you.

But, in 2012, before the publication of Mr. Lewis's book, you mentioned that there were many investors that were sort of turned off by the casino-type environment that they sensed, rightly or wrongly, and your clients, has that distrust, mistrust, or cynicism grown in the last 2 years?

Mr. BROOKS. I do not know whether it has grown, but I also do not think it has abated. So, you know, we talked about the percentage of the households in this country that have exposure to the stocks at sort of 16-year lows and the millennials. I do not know what draws people to a market or away from investing, but that is not a good thing. You cannot save for your retirement if you do not generate some sort of return. So, we are pretty concerned about this whole issue.

The job of trying to affirm a market's reasonableness, its fairness, its transparency, seems to us to be ongoing, and we have sort of—we are not doing a good enough job there collectively as an industry and everybody to try and affirm the reasonableness and fairness of our market. So, we continue to be concerned about that issue.

Senator REED. I think everyone has commented that high frequency trading has provided some significant advantages to marketplace liquidity, and in some cases probably narrowing price spreads, et cetera, but, again, going to particularly this popular perception argument that some of it seems to be algorithms that are cleverly designed to essentially not make economic investments, but to exploit sort of timing gaps in the system and other gaps in the system. You know, one of the things that is referred to is the sort of algorithms that will send out a huge number of bids and then cancel the bids, not because of the market activity, just simply because that is how they think they can move a price just a few basis points and then make the right move. That seems to me to be behavior that does not add to the economic value of the country, but it certainly makes some people very wealthy.

Mr. BROOKS. We would agree with that, and sort of following up on what Professor Scott was talking about, intraday volatility, institutional investors who are really aggregated retail—it is everybody together, because that is who we represent—we do care about intraday volatility because it is in that environment that we are trading. It is in that environment that we are making our investment to hold something for 5 years. And, if a trading strategy—if someone has been able to exacerbate that volatility between 9:30 and 4, I would argue it is causing longer-term investors a higher cost.

Senator Warren sort of talked about a tax. That is sort of a tax on the system. All the money that the high frequency crowd is taking out—they are not taking risk overnight, they are flat every day, they never lose money—all the profits they are making are coming from someone else. That might be the longer-term investors, everybody in their 401(k)s, their 529 plans, et cetera.

So, we are very concerned about intraday volatility and that is why we would like to see some pilot programs to examine, can we constrain that a little bit? Can we make the markets a little deeper, a little more transparent to bring that intraday volatility in, narrow it? We do not have the answer until we try.

Mr. SOLOMON. We agree with that——

Senator REED. Let me go to Mr. Solomon, and then I will ask Professor Scott just to comment on the general sort of discussion that we have initiated with Mr. Brooks. Mr. Solomon.

Mr. SOLOMON. Yes, Senator. We agree completely. Actually, we are very much on the same side here. The intraday volatility in single stocks has actually, in some instances, never been higher. When a buyer shows up, the stock lifts inexplicably, and when a seller shows up, the stock drops inexplicably. So, I do not really think there are a lot of good measures for single stock volatility.

I think, with all due respect to the Professor, I do not think the VIX has anything to do with this. The VIX is an irrelevant—it just looks at overall market volatility and all it says is that, you know, generally speaking, people are, you know, sanguine about the overall market, in general, macroeconomically, even with all the worries. They are generally sanguine. When they are not sanguine, the VIX will be 40. But, it does not impact what happens in single stocks.

There are some definite issues here that are exacerbated by the market structure, and high frequency—some high frequency traders that do engage in flash trading behavior, in particular, are harmful, I mean, and I do not think there is anybody that can argue about that.

But, if you look at the reason why people flash, it is because a lot of the trading goes on in the dark. So, dark pools are, by their definition, not transparent. So, if you want to trade in a dark pool, well, you need a way to light that dark pool, and one of the ways you can light that dark pool is by flash trading and seeing where the bids and offers are. And, the question is whether or not dark pool operators encourage that kind of behavior or discourage that kind of behavior.

At Cowen, we do not run a dark pool and we are not interested in running a dark pool. We have access to a lot of different liquidity providers and we have developed algorithms to help folks like Andy access pockets of liquidity and combat that kind of behavior. So, there are some market clearing mechanisms that allow you to deal with that. But, in general, if you do not have the kind of algorithms we have to combat that kind of behavior, you are at a significant disadvantage.

I would also say, when people talk about speed, there are plenty of analogies we could use about speed and what it does. We can all say that the National Highway System increased the productivity of this country in ways that even President Eisenhower could not imagine. But, we have speed limits. Every car on the highway can go faster than it is allowed to go. So, it is OK for regulators and legislators to say, we know you can go faster. We know you can make improvements in efficiencies of your engines. But, we think that this is the right speed to encourage the right kind of economic behavior and protect investors.

So, I do not think you are actually being a Luddite at all by asking the question, just because we can go faster, should we go faster, and there are plenty of examples like that one that suggest we might not be better.

Senator REED. Thank you. Thank you very much. Just a last word, if I may prevail upon my colleagues.

Senator JOHANNS. Sure. Go ahead.

Senator REED. Thank you, Mike.

Professor, please. And, welcome. Good to see you.

Mr. SCOTT. Thank you, Senator. I think we need to keep our eye on the ball. The ball is, you know, what is best for people who are trading in this market and what do they care about, and in turn, what is best for our economy? So, we talked about three different elements in the market. We talked about volatility. We talked about liquidity. We talked about transaction costs. OK.

So, on volatility, I have already said, people disagree on this. It depends how you measure volatility, OK. I still am of the view where maybe traders get rewarded for a little less volatility during the day. Does a long-term investor really care about intraday volatility? The people who are trading for them may care because they get compensated on basically how they do. But, for the long-term investor, I have to say, I am in TIAA–CREF and I could care less about intraday market volatility.

Now, the second part of it is liquidity, OK. People are obviously interested in being able to trade in and out of their stock positions when they want to. This is retail and institutional. And, here again, we have a lot of data, all right, an economist that says, liquidity overall in this market is an all-time best. And, yet, Jeff, OK, when he deals with small cap stocks, he does not see that because we are measuring the overall market, which is dominated by large cap stocks. So, if we have a liquidity problem, I think it is targeted—should be targeted, and I think Jeff would agree with this, at trying to get more liquidity in small cap stocks. We do not have that liquidity. Therefore, people do not want to invest in them. Therefore, we do not have capital formation.

And, the third thing is transaction costs, and this goes back to Senator Johanns' questions or observations. You know, retail costs, I think everybody would agree, are at an all-time low. Nobody here, I think, has said that is not the case. On the institutional side, we have studies by financial economists—there was just a recent study by Angel, Harris, Chester Spatt, they are all pretty well recognized financial economists, who say the average transaction cost for an institutional order of one million shares for a $30 stock is at a historic low of 40 basis points, OK. So, we have to reconcile that conclusion with what Mr. Brooks is observing. I am not saying Mr. Brooks is not observing higher transaction costs, but here is a pretty well respected group of financial economists who are saying it is at an all-time low.

So, I come back to Senator Johanns' process question, really. There are a lot of differences of opinions on these issues, OK, and it is, in my view, the SEC's first role to sort this out, write a good report for our country, including for this Committee or for the greater Senate Committee and the House, and then we will have something, OK, to look at and react to.

So, I think, again, we should not be legislating now on these issues. We should be fact finding and the primary fact finder should be the SEC. And, by the way, Senator Reed, when you were out of the room, I am very much in favor of the SEC having adequate funding to do this and other things.

Senator REED. Thank you very much. Thank you, gentlemen.

Senator JOHANNS. Go ahead.

Mr. BROOKS. Could I possibly respond to——

Senator JOHANNS. Mr. Brooks, you wanted to——

Mr. BROOKS. So, there are lots of studies out there talking about transaction costs, and you can pretty much find a study to match any opinion you want to espouse. There is an RBC study out saying that intraday volatility costs are now perhaps higher than ever, and we are seeing that in our trading. And, I know Professor Angel and he is a good guy and he does good work, but it depends what you are examining, and so that is a very complicated subject, too, talking about transaction costs.

Two other things we have all sort of talked about here today are conflicts of interest and complexity, and we could be better if we could eliminate conflicts of interest and reduce complexity, and I want to just tell you a quick story, a trading story.

So, one day a few years ago, T. Rowe Price, we had 2.5 million shares to trade in a number of different stocks and we picked a broker and they were about our number 7th broker on the day in terms of the business we did. That 2.5 million shares got represented out to the marketplace as 750 million shares of interest, 300-to-one. So, we had 2.5 million shares to buy. It got displayed in different times, different ways, as 750 million shares, simply to get 2.5 million shares executed.

Now, was that a great trading strategy? The numbers looked pretty good. The reality is, we have 11 exchanges and 50-plus dark pools. That complexity, that myriad of—that spider web out there of where you have to go to trade today has created all kinds of challenges for every investor, and it is that issue that we need to try and focus on. How crazy is it that you have to go to so many different places to say, anybody there? Anybody want to trade? Anybody care today? We are really—we are obfuscating things, and people have been able to figure out ways to profit from that that really cause them to take no risk.

Mr. SOLOMON. I am willing to bet that that was a large capitalization stock, too.

Mr. BROOKS. They were across the spectrum, actually.

Mr. SOLOMON. Right. And, so, if you look at what happens in small cap stocks—sometimes, you know, it is like—we call it the Hotel California. If you own a small cap stock, you can check out any time you like, but you can never leave. And, that is a problem when it comes to capital formation.

And, we talk—prior to the JOBS Act, which was to get companies to think about going public, private companies, we seem to have established a really good regime in the Congress where we can do good legislation that balances investor protections and creates a forum for capital formation. But, once these companies are public, who is actually sponsoring them and how is that trading occurring?

And, we are in a period now where we have a number of new companies, and we would love to give them the right kind of experience to encourage further investment in capital-intensive businesses from your venture capital friends who right now, if you look at the last 10 years of venture capital investment in this country, it is disproportionately in companies that do not hire lots of people, or are not capital intensive. We do not back semiconductor manufacturing companies in this country anymore. That is a problem.

And, so, if you need access to capital beyond the venture spectrum, you have to find it in the public markets, and this is what we are talking about. There needs to be that liquidity.

Chairman WARNER. Senator Johanns gets his question.

Senator JOHANNS. Maybe more of an observation than a question, and here would be my observation. I came to this hearing today wondering about the process question—that is why I asked it first out of the box—just simply because we, years and years ago, created an SEC. We gave them authorities. We have looked at that from time to time. We have broadened their authority and we have said to them, we want you to be the experts. We want you to understand this marketplace and report to us on what is working and what is not working.

And, I leave this hearing today more and more convinced that if there is direction from Congress, it should be direction to the SEC to go out there and find the facts, report back, do the pilot program—which, incidentally, I have no problem with.

The second observation is this. What traders are doing is not illegal. If they are out there buying and selling and doing what they are doing within the laws that are currently on the books, they have a right to do that. And, it occurs to me, Mr. Brooks, that they have kind of outsmarted you, not because you are less intelligent than they are, but they watch you like a hawk and all of a sudden they are starting to figure some things out and they are just a second ahead of you and it is profitable.

Now, I would not be smart enough to do that. I guess if I were that smart, I would be doing that instead of what I am doing now, right?

Chairman WARNER. You are not running for reelection, though, right?

Senator JOHANNS. Yes.

[Laughter.]

Senator JOHANNS. I will not be doing that in my next life.

All I am saying to you is before we head out there in a free marketplace and start defining behavior to be illegal, we should be darn sure about what we are doing, because it could have some economic consequences.

Now, I want you to go out and give me the very best deal, and I do not think I am invested in your company whatsoever, but I do have a retirement program here that I have got some money in, and I tell you what, I look at the statement and I say, way to go. Good job. You are making more money for me. I want you to do that.

But, having said that, again, I think we need to be very thoughtful about when we proclaim behavior to be illegal in a free market system, and that one, I must admit, I want more information on. I want more fact finding. I want to understand who wins, who loses, what is the consequences. And, I do not think we are anywhere near there at this point.

Like I said, I leave this hearing with somewhat the same impression I came to the hearing with, and that is we need the SEC out there to lead this effort. We need to encourage them, fund them, do those things. And then a future Congress—this will happen after I am gone—needs to be careful and thoughtful about how they are going to figure this out, because just because they are making money does not warrant us jumping in and saying, that behavior is illegal. You are making money. That has got to be illegal behavior.

Mr. BROOKS. Senator, I think that is a—your point is well made. I do not think we are saying this behavior is illegal, but it might not be fair. It might not be right. It might not be ethical. So, if someone gets an information advantage about my trade and they get it—they get knowledge of a trade that is going to happen, and it happens and they are able to profit from that knowledge before the rest of the market can, when it is really marketwide knowledge that should be shared, I am not sure that advantage is right.

I have no problem with people making money. I mean, we are a for-profit enterprise. This is America. We believe in that. But, when you take an unfair advantage or you found an unfair advantage and you have exploited that, I think that maybe the SEC needs to gut-check that and come back and say, maybe we can tweak things, because that is not fair.

That is why I think the tax loophole analogy is a good one. You know, we respect people that found ways to avoid paying taxes, but if it is a loophole, it often needs to be closed. And, we think that some of these predatory practices are, in fact, not fair and not right and they should not be allowed to go on. It is not that they are illegal, but they have an unfair advantage.

You know, my mother used to say to me, ''Just because you can do it does not mean it is right,'' and I think that is important.

Senator JOHANNS. You know, and I got the same lesson.

Mr. BROOKS. Yes, sir.

Senator JOHANNS. I got the same lesson, and I do not agree with the philosophy you espouse, and I hope I live by that philosophy. But, again, highly technical, critical that we get good information from the SEC, critical that we understand what the consequences of our actions might be, because at the end of the day, there will be consequences. And what we stop here may open something up over here that we do not like any better. Like I said, I just think we need to be very careful, very thoughtful.

I have not read the book. I am sure it is a great read. Mr. Lewis is a fascinating author. But, having said that, this is very serious business, and if there is anything I take from this hearing and three outstanding panelists, in my judgment, is we need to be thoughtful about where we head from here.

Mr. SOLOMON. This is why we have advocated for pilots. I think if there is one consensus, we have all said that there should be pilots and we should observe those pilots and make changes based on the information we gather from that.

I will just say, there is a little bit of a difference at the SEC now than there was when the JOBS Act was passed. Chairwoman White has really made this a priority. She is data-driven. She is going to do a lot of analytics. And, she has been very consistent in her commentary, as have the other Commissioners. So, I do think that we can maybe get some answers from them.

But, I will say that the first thing that came out that was required—the JOBS Act required the SEC to look at market structure, and I would encourage you to read that report and see if you learned anything from that. And, I would say, part of the reason why we formed the Equity Capital Formation Task Force is we looked at that report and said, it did not tell us anything. So, we have to advocate for them to actually tell us something that is helpful.

And, I am hopeful that under this leadership of Chairwoman White that we will get a different outcome, but I think it is Congress' responsibility to ensure that we get that output, and that is part of the reason why I am here, at least.

Chairman WARNER. Let me—and, again, I appreciate everybody's comments and, I think, the very good questions. And, I think, Senator Johanns and I have worked on a lot of things together. We get the conflict. We have got the value-add to the economy of the retail investor being able to get that cheaper price.

But, I do think the notion, and I am a proud free market advocate and proud of my experience longer in business than I have been in politics, but there is this notion in the market, you take risks and you take your lumps and you take your wins. Something that is inherently—a track record that says if 99.9 percent of the days in a trading exchange you make money—and it is not just an HFT, I recall some of the large cap banks who had those same records—it creates at least something that is echoing what you have said. We need more data.

And, I come back to the fact, May 13, not May 13 in 2010, but May 13 in 2014, Xerox and Lorillard, this was the—we had a miniflash crash. And, if we were to have another one of these incidents, the tendency would be, as you know, Senator, we might overreact too quickly. So, the fact that we are 4 years after the first Flash Crash—and I remember the previous Chair of the SEC, asking her what happened, and months and months later, they were still trying to find out—the fact that we do not have that consolidated audit trail information done—I mean, I am for adequate funding for the SEC, as well, but at some point, the priority—this needs to be a higher priority. And, I do think we have a role to nudge the SEC to act, to make this a higher priority, to urge our colleagues on both sides of the aisle to get the SEC the resources they need to do their job, number one.

I think, at least, I, and I think you have concurred on the tick size, the pilot, the notion of small caps. We want to try to accelerate that.

But, there are—I think Mr. Brooks has raised some fundamental questions about this notion of fairness here that we do not have all the appropriate data to kind of make that judgment. And, my concern will be, if we do not have that data soon, another incident will happen, and, my gosh, because of the complexity, Congress trying to line-by-line legislate this would not be a pretty activity.

All right, Professor Scott. Briefly, because we are about to bring the hearing to an end.

Mr. Scott. I just want to put in a plug. Our committee has got a full-scale project to examine all these market structure issues and we will be doing so over the next 9 months. So, I want to say, the SEC is not the only organization out there that is going to be studying market structure. Our committee is doing it. I am sure there will be others for you to look at and sort of weigh those other studies against whatever the SEC——

Chairman Warner. And, I would say this. One of the things I think this Subcommittee needs to do, since we have this as our jurisdiction, and Senator Levin had some of the folks yesterday, but, you know, we need to have some folks—back to Mr. Brooks' point about how many exchanges there are out there competing, it should be very, very small. You would have to search out these very, very small exchanges. On the other hand, in the notion of a market, they need to have their say in this Committee, as well.

I want to thank all the witnesses for very focused answers and appreciate your contribution. Senator Johanns, thanks for your contribution, as well.

The hearing is adjourned.

[Whereupon, at 11:29 a.m., the hearing was adjourned.]

[Prepared statements and additional material supplied for the record follow:]

PREPARED STATEMENT OF HAL S. SCOTT

NOMURA PROFESSOR AND DIRECTOR, PROGRAM ON INTERNATIONAL FINANCIAL
SYSTEMS, HARVARD LAW SCHOOL

JUNE 18, 2014

Thank you, Chairman Warner, Ranking Member Johanns, and Members of the Subcommittee for permitting me to testify before you today on the impact of high frequency trading on investor confidence and capital formation in U.S. equity markets. I am testifying in my own capacity and do not purport to represent the views of any organizations with which I am affiliated, although some of my testimony is based on the work of the Committee on Capital Markets Regulation (CCMR). On the whole, high frequency-trading increases liquidity in our equity capital markets. The increased liquidity leads to decreased costs of stock issuance, thus improving capital formation. And of course, improved capital formation for our businesses leads to higher growth in the real economy.

The Committee was formed in 2005 to address the issue of competitiveness in our primary public equity capital markets and issued a report in 2006 detailing the threats to our primary markets and suggestions for improvement.[1] Just as regulatory changes can lead to competitiveness concerns in our primary markets, the same is true of our secondary markets. Therefore, any changes in our secondary market trading must be assessed for their competitive implications, particularly given the current relative competitive strength of our secondary markets vis-a-vis those abroad.

The CCMR tracks, on a quarterly basis, 13 measures of the competitiveness of the U.S. public equity market.[2] We have found that while the competitiveness of our primary markets has suffered over the past 6 years, our secondary markets remain strong with roughly 50 percent of global exchange trading occurring on U.S. exchanges.[3] The CCMR is currently undertaking a review of market structure issues with a focus on dark pools, internalization, decimalization, exchange backup systems, and the subject of today's hearings, high frequency trading.

"High frequency trading" or "HFT" is a topic that has generated significant attention in recent years and increasingly in the last few months. The widespread public interest in this topic was intensified following the 2010 "flash crash" and more recently, with the publication of Michael Lewis' book *Flash Boys,* which has ignited a general attack on HFT's place in the U.S. capital markets. But policy cannot be made on the basis of a journalistic tale that makes for a best seller—rather it must be informed by verifiable facts. This is largely why we are here today and my intention is to provide a thoughtful response to a debate that has been at times fraught with frenzied emotion.

Let me be clear at the outset, that I believe the net effect of HFT activity in our equity markets has been positive. Transaction costs are at historic lows, liquidity is at historic highs, and volatility has stabilized. These features of today's market not only benefit both retail and institutional investors, but also positively affect capital formation, and by extension, promote job creation. The fact that HFT is the subject of a best-selling book and has generated vocal opposition both within the financial industry and across the American public more broadly, does not, in itself, justify drastic regulatory change. There is nothing new about the advantages of speed to traders. You may recall that the Rothschilds used carrier pigeons to bring them news of the outcome of battles in the Napoleonic wars.[4] While the speed with which they obtained this information gave the Rothschilds an advantage, the markets generally benefited from the speed by which the new information got into the market, even if those who actually traded with the Rothschilds were at a disadvantage.

My primary concern is that the recent frenzy over HFTs draws attention away from other important market structure issues. For example, as a member of the Equity Capital Formation Task Force, along with my fellow panelist Mr. Solomon, I have been highly supportive of a tick-size pilot program for small cap stocks and have been encouraged by the SEC's recent commitment to conduct such a program.[5]

---

[1] Comm. On Capital Mkts. Reg., Interim Report of the Committee on Capital Markets Regulation (Nov. 30, 2006), *http://www.capmktsreg.org/pdfs/11.30Committee\Interim\ReportREV2pdf.*
[2] Comm. on Capital Mkts. Reg., Competitiveness Measures, *http://www.capmktsreg.org/educationresearch/competitiveness-measures/*
[3] Id.
[4] Mary Blume, "The Hallowed History of the Carrier Pigeon", *New York Times,* Jan. 30, 2004.
[5] See Letter from Hal S. Scott to Joseph Dear, Chairman, Inv. Adv. Comm., U.S. Sec. and Exch. Comm. (Jan. 23, 2014), available at *http://www.equitycapitalformationtaskforce.com/files/H%20Scott%20IAC%20letter%202014%2001%2023.pdf.*

That being said, to the extent that public concern over HFTs reduces investor confidence, our capital markets will suffer. But in my opinion, any reduction in confidence would not be based on the facts. Given the recent volumes in trading, there is little evidence that people have lost confidence in our markets.

Critics of HFT point to the $261 billion that retail investors have pulled from equity mutual funds since the 2010 "flash crash" as evidence that investors have lost confidence in our equity markets.[6] However, retail investors have simply moved their investments to exchange traded products, which of course trade in U.S. equity markets. The net effect is investor inflows of almost $500 billion since the 2010 flash crash.[7] In 2012 alone, there were net inflows of $57 billion in securities trading in U.S. equity markets.[8] If investors were indeed overly concerned by HFT then they wouldn't have added such substantial amounts to their capital at risk in our equity markets.

Another common misconception regarding HFT and our current equity market structure is that HFTs have somehow caused an increase in transaction costs for individual retail investors. In fact, transaction costs for retail investors are at historic lows, as evidenced by current bid-ask spreads and retail brokerage commissions. Since 2006, the average effective bid-ask spread on NYSE-listed stocks has dropped in half, from over 3 cents to roughly 1.5.[9] Retail brokerage commissions are also at all-time lows; the average commission charged by the three major retail brokers is approximately $10 per trade.[10] Given the reduction in spreads and commissions, the net cost of a given trade has dropped dramatically for retail investors. According to the Tabb Group, 7 years ago retail investors' effective payments on executed trades were roughly 130 percent of the NBBO spread (the difference between the national best bid and offer). Since then they have dropped to less than 100 percent, so the average retail investor receives a better price on a trade than the best price available on an exchange.[11] In short, it is a great time to be a retail investor.

However, bear in mind that retail investors only directly account for approximately 15–20 percent of daily stock market volume.[12] Since many retail investors access the equity markets indirectly through institutional funds or advisors (such as mutual funds, pension funds, or private wealth advisors), institutional cost reduction is highly relevant to retail investors as well. In 1950, over 90 percent of U.S. equities were held directly by households.[13] That number has dropped to less than 40 percent in 2013[14] and this is primarily high-net worth individuals. Household ownership of mutual funds has risen from 5.7 percent in 1980 to 46.3 percent in 2013 constituting 90 percent of mutual fund assets.[15] Collectively mutual funds own 30 percent of the U.S. stock market capitalization.[16] Clearly, what is good for institutional investors is also beneficial for the small investor.

The institutional investors that primarily trade on behalf of the small investor constitute roughly 25–35 percent of average daily stock trading volume in the U.S.[17] And today institutional trading costs are historically low. Based on institutional trade data compiled by leading finance academics, the average transaction cost for an institutional order of 1 million shares for a $30 stock is at a historic low of 40 basis points.[18] This includes additional costs associated with price movement from information leakage. The costs of trading these large orders can exceed bid/ask spreads if there is information leakage that a large order is being placed and the price of the trade subsequently moves against the buyer. To prevent this, institutional traders split large orders into small orders for execution to avoid tipping off other market participants that a large order has entered the market. Neither retail nor institutional investors appear to have suffered from the increase in HFT trading

[6] Justin Schack, "HFT Is Not Driving Investors From the Stock Market", *Fin. Times,* May 10, 2013.

[7] Id.

[8] Id.

[9] See James J. Angel, Lawrence E. Harris, and Chester S. Spatt, "Equity Trading in the 21st Century: An Update", June 21, 2013.

[10] Id.

[11] See "The Citadel Conversation", Q1 2013, available at *https://www.citadelsecurities.com/lfiles/uploads/sites/2/2013/06/The-Citadel-Conversation-with-Larry-Tabb-and-Jamil-Nazarali.pdf.*

[12] Rosenblatt Securities estimate.

[13] B. Friedman, "Economic Implications of Changing Share Ownership", *Journal of Portfolio Management* 22 (Spring 1996).

[14] Board of Governors of the Federal Reserve System, Flow-of-Funds Accounts (2013).

[15] Investment Company Institute, 2013 Factbook.

[16] Id.

[17] Rosenblatt Securities estimate.

[18] See James J. Angel, Lawrence E. Harris, and Chester S. Spatt, "Equity Trading in the 21st Century: An Update", June 21, 2013.

activity. If anything, market participants are experiencing the best trading conditions ever seen.

In addition to transaction costs, market volatility and more importantly severe market dislocations are also a primary concern for all investors. Critics of HFT contend that HFT strategies have led to a significant increase in stock market volatility caused merely by HFT trading activity, rather than changes to the fundamentals of stocks. However, respected market structure experts continue to believe that volatility is largely driven by macroeconomic concerns and not HFT activity. Stock market volatility, as proxied by the CBOE Volatility Index (VIX), understandably rose during the heart of the financial crisis, but has since fallen to its lowest levels in seven years. Intraday volatility of individual stocks also remains low. Professor Larry Harris has found that there is no clear pattern that stock market volatility or the intraday volatility of individual stocks has accompanied the rise of HFT. [19] And while the extreme volatility experienced during the flash crash in 2010 was a significant market disruption that should not be repeated, the SEC has largely addressed this concern by implementing single-stock circuit breakers and revising marketwide circuit breakers that will temporarily halt trading if price movements become too volatile.

Thus, it is hard to argue that the U.S. equity market is "broken" as a result of the emergence of HFT activity. Nonetheless, there is always room for targeted improvement of the current regulatory structure, including with respect to certain practices of HFT traders. But we should proceed cautiously and thoughtfully so as not to chill legitimate market functions. There are risks to implementing any changes which must be assessed—for example, bid/offer spreads could widen or exchange volumes (and with it liquidity) could drop.

As a first step, we must precisely identify what practices warrant further regulatory scrutiny. Defining high frequency trading is far from straightforward. For example, many institutional traders place relatively small trades with high frequency, but whether this is a unique and potentially abusive investment strategy or whether this is simply an optimal trading strategy that has evolved with automated trading (e.g., to execute a large block trade without exposing the size of the order), is a baseline question. Technological advances mean that modern trading is done electronically with orders no longer being given to a broker on an exchange floor. And trading is getting faster every year. We can't put the genie back in the bottle; Mary Jo White recently acknowledged that "the SEC should not roll back the technology clock." [20]

At the same time, there are certainly many general risks that come with automated and faster trading. We need to make sure our rules keep up with industry technology. Regulation has not kept pace with technological advances. As Mary Jo White acknowledged, "many market structure rules and industry practices were developed with manual markets in mind." [21] We have seen other significant changes in response to modern technology before—for example, following the October '87 crash, when the NYSE implemented marketwide circuit breakers in response to the recommendations of a presidential task force. [22]

Market instability is something everyone agrees we need to avoid, to the extent possible. In our fast-paced world, our markets are particularly susceptible both to fat finger mistakes and errors, as well as intentional, manipulative behavior by certain market participants. The incredible speed at which we now trade can exacerbate errors, and quickly.

We need to ensure the safety and soundness of our markets. Fortunately, as I have previously mentioned, the SEC and securities industry have already taken a number of steps to address this topic. For example, in addition to circuit breakers, the SEC has issued requirements for market participants to address technology risks through the Market Access Rule and proposed Regulation SCI. The Consolidated Audit Trail is expected to be operational in 2016 and will provide the SEC comprehensive data regarding the routing and execution of orders, allowing regulators to better prevent, identify and respond to any firms engaged in harmful practices.

Critics of HFT contend that HFT firms have access to proprietary data feeds from the exchanges that provide them with information before other traders, allowing

---

[19] Id.

[20] Mary Jo White, Chair, U.S. Sec. and Exch. Comm., "Enhancing Our Equity Market Structure", Speech at Sandler O'Neill & Partners, L.P. Global Exchange and Brokerage Conference (Jun. 5, 2014).

[21] Id.

[22] See NYSE Circuit Breakers, available at *https://usequities.nyx.com/markets/nyse-equities/circuitbreakers.*

them to "front run" the market. However, it is important to be clear that trading on information that is publicly available is different than a broker trading ahead of a customer, which is patently illegal. Michael Lewis points out examples in which he claims that HFT traders obtain an advantage in the market when brokers trade only a small portion of a larger customer order with the HFT to gain a rebate on that small portion. The HFT then uses the information from the small order to trade ahead of the remainder of the customer's order, thus resulting in the broker's customer receiving an inferior price for the remainder of the order. However, the flaw in these examples is that brokers actually route customer orders in a manner that ensures that their customers' orders arrive at various trading platforms at the exact same time, so customers receive the best price for their full order. Such routing practices are consistent with brokers' legal requirement to seek the best execution reasonably available for their customers' orders. Specific examples are described in the appendix.

Additionally, there is growing public interest in a practice called "colocation," which refers to traders locating their data servers in the same physical space as exchanges to facilitate faster trading and profits, which along with proprietary data feeds gave rise to latency arbitrage. In general, latency arbitrage entails the ability of HFTs to synthesize quotes from all exchanges faster than other market participants, thus enabling HFTs to trade on those quotes at a profit. One could argue that this activity closes the gap between divergent prices in similar ways as other forms of arbitrage. While critics question the "fairness" of allowing certain traders to benefit from their physical proximity to an exchange or access to proprietary data feeds, proponents of the practice point out that the SEC does not allow exchanges to discriminate in offering these services. If an exchange offers proprietary data feeds or colocation to any traders, it is required to offer access to all other market participants, both HFT firms and non-HFT firms, at the same cost. Under this system, every market participant has an opportunity to colocate. If the exchanges no longer offered this access to anyone, either by choice or prohibition, a race would ensue to acquire the real estate adjacent to the exchange, which could actually limit access to many market participants. One might even view colocation as the modern incarnation of market makers vying for position on an exchange floor. Furthermore, 90 percent of all trades are now executed by colocated traders with access to proprietary data feeds, which includes institutional investors acting on behalf of retail investors. [23]

Another issue to consider is the increasing technology "arms race" occurring among HFTs. To beat out competitors, HFTs invest more heavily in powerful and expensive technology to gain an edge over the competition. But increased competition among HFTs may further reduce costs for the rest of the market as HFT margins decline. The TABB Group estimates that HFT revenues in the U.S. have dropped from $7.2 billion in 2009 to $1.3 billion in 2014. [24]

Much discussion recently has also revolved around the "maker-taker" pricing system that developed roughly 17 years ago, well before the rise of HFTs. [25] On a trading platform with "maker-taker" pricing, the liquidity taker pays a fee and the liquidity provider receives a rebate. The first venue to introduce maker-taker pricing was Island ECN in 1997. [26] While some have introduced various criticisms of maker-taker pricing, this is neither a system nor a problem created by HFTs. The maker-taker pricing system can exist in low frequency trading environments and HFT environments alike.

Finally, I note that certain critics of HFTs are also highly critical of the "dark pools" where these traders, along with other institutional investors, increasingly trade. It is estimated that 15 percent of stocks are now executed in dark pools, where information about orders is not publicly displayed. [27] Critics suggest that dark trading inhibits the pricing function of secondary markets, and also question their opacity more generally. It is important to note, however, that neither dark pools nor market fragmentation more generally are "problems" that arose because of HFT. The automation of equity trading following the SEC's adoption of Regulation National Market System (Reg NMS) in 2005 led to a fragmentation of execution venues, including SEC registered exchanges as well as alternative trading venues like dark pools. Thus dark pools and fragmentation were partly the result of regula-

---

[23] Rosenblatt Securities estimate.

[24] TABB Forum, "No, Michael Lewis, the U.S. Equities Market Is Not Rigged", *http://tabforum.com/opinions/no-michael-lewis-the-us-equities-market-is-not-rigged.*

[25] See Larry Harris, "Maker-Taker Pricing Effects on Market Quotations", Aug. 30, 2013.

[26] Id.

[27] James J. Angel, Lawrence E. Harris, and Chester S. Spatt, "Equity Trading in the 21st Century: An Update", June 21, 2013.

tion. In addition though, there were general market forces at work. Buy-side traders who questioned whether their trades were being front-run on traditional exchanges turned to dark pools because of the protection that dark trading brings from potential front-running. One key benefit to dark pools is that orders are not displayed, thus it is difficult to front-run them or to know when large blocks are being bid and offered. Furthermore, it is important to remember that a Reg NMS stock can only be traded in the dark if it is executed at a price that is equal to or better than the best publicly available price on an exchange. In addition, dark pools are required to offer post-trade transparency, as executed stocks are publicly reported in real time. While proposals to further reform dark pools, for example, by requiring disclosure of trading practices or fee structures or imposing antidiscrimination rules, may warrant further attention, such reforms are unrelated to HFT and outside the scope of my testimony today.

I would now like to present a few specific proposals that I believe could be helpful in ensuring the safety and security of our automated world.

First, regulators should consider mandating and harmonizing exchange-level kill switches. A kill switch is a mechanism that would halt a firm's trading activity when a preestablished exposure threshold has been breached, thus stopping erroneous orders and preventing any further uncontrolled accumulation of positions. For example, if a trading firm typically only holds $1,000,000 in shares of NASDAQ-traded stock during any point in the trading day, it could be required to implement a kill switch at 5 times that exposure-level, or $5,000,000 in shares of NASDAQ-traded stocks. If the threshold is breached, further trading would be prevented and the firm's open orders on NASDAQ would be halted. It is important that such kill switches be mandatory at the exchange level. This would serve to further mitigate volatility related to errant algorithms or "fat finger" errors.

Second, we might consider addressing the volume of order message traffic, which can create market instability, by establishing order-to-trade ratios. Electronic order instructions are used to direct the placement, cancellation and correction of orders. Since 2005, order flow has increased by 1,000 percent while trade volume has increased by only 20 percent.[28] As was experienced during the 2010 flash crash, a spike in orders and cancellations can exacerbate market volatility and overwhelm the exchanges' infrastructure. The current market structure only places costs on trade executions, thereby allowing market participants to generate excessive order-message traffic without internalizing the costs of the negative externalities just described. Regulators should assess why order volumes have increased and consider charging fees for extreme message traffic, keeping in mind that any order-to-trade ratios should depend on the liquidity of the stock.

Third, regulators should consider abolishing immunity that exchanges have from liabilities for losses from market disruptions based on their SRO status. For example, NASDAQ received immunity from liability for half-a-billion dollars of losses incurred by brokers from the Facebook trading glitch because it claimed it was acting in its SRO, and not its for-profit, capacity. If immunity does not apply to activities related to smart routing and other technology offerings, this might better align the exchanges' incentives to limit potentially risky trading activity that could pose widespread operational risk.

In addition to the proposals discussed above, I wanted to address two recent suggestions by Mary Jo White. First, the SEC staff is working to develop a recommendation for an antidisruptive trading rule.[29] In theory, such a rule has potential as a targeted solution aimed at aggressive short-term traders. However, "the devil is in the details." While such a rule would be aimed at active proprietary traders during specific, short time periods when the markets are most vulnerable, basic questions will need to be addressed, such as which traders should be restricted, during which time periods, and for which activities. There may be some clear-cut cases, where for instance it would be easy to craft a rule that says: "don't short further during a period where stock's value has declined by x." But it is perhaps not as clear-cut as to whether we should impose an affirmative market-making obligation during periods of stress. None of this is to say an antidisruptive trading rule is undesirable; however, it would need to be formulated carefully.

---

[28] See Gary Cohn, Op-Ed, "The Responsible Way To Rein in Super-Fast Trading", *Wall Street Journal*, Mar. 20, 2014; and James J. Angel, Lawrence E. Harris, and Chester S. Spatt, "Equity Trading in the 21st Century: An Update", June 21, 2013.

[29] See Mary Jo White, Chair, U.S. Sec. and Exch. Comm., "Enhancing Our Equity Market Structure", Speech at Sandler O'Neill & Partners, L.P. Global Exchange and Brokerage Conference (Jun. 5, 2014).

White has also asked her staff to propose a recommendation that would subject unregistered active proprietary traders to the SEC's rule as dealers.[30] Again, such a rule could potentially be an effective tool in monitoring and regulating the behavior of harmful trading practices. But it may be difficult to identify which "unregistered active proprietary traders" should be subject to broker-dealer requirements. We have seen similar difficulties in the new practice of designating "swap dealers" under Dodd-Frank. Furthermore, a number of these entities may be subject to oversight already. The SEC should ensure that any registration requirements are streamlined and coordinated.

Finally, I'd like to address the topic of decimalization. As I mentioned up front, I eagerly await the specifics of the SEC's pilot program on tick sizes. I would hope that the SEC pays particular attention when applying different metrics to different types of securities covered by the program, so as not to introduce additional operational risk through increasingly complex trading rules for these stocks. For example, I understand the SEC is considering dividing the pilot into three groups of stocks, which trade at different increments and may or may not be subject to the "trade at" rule.[31] I encourage the SEC to keep in mind the safety and soundness of our equity markets when finalizing the design for this pilot.

Thank you and I look forward to your questions.

APPENDIX

The following are specific examples of allegedly predatory trading behavior by HFTs from *Flash Boys*. I follow with a response to the perceived problem posed by the example.

Example 1: On pages 74–75, the example has a customer wishing to purchase 100,000 shares of XYZ Company at $25 per share. In this example, 100 shares are offered on BATS for $25 and 10,000 shares are offered by other sellers on each of ten more exchanges. Lewis suggests that the broker's router will send the buy order to BATS first to receive a rebate offered by BATS, even though BATS is only offering 100 shares. However, the problem then arises that once the BATS trade is executed, the other 100,000 shares available may disappear before they can be purchased.

This example fails to recognize how brokers actually route customer trades in order to satisfy their "best execution" requirement, which precedes Reg NMS. In practice, brokers will send orders to acquire the 100 shares on BATS and 10,000 shares on the ten other exchanges at the same time. In fact, brokers have flexibility to actually send the order for 100,000 shares of XYZ Company to the other exchanges slightly before they send the 100 share order to BATS, if the broker reasonably believes this will achieve a lower fill price for the customer's complete order for XYZ Company.

Example 2: On pages 137–138, the example has a customer wishing to purchase shares of IBM through a broker (Goldman Sachs in this example) In this example, the broker is required to purchase 100 shares on BATS for $19.99 before purchasing 500 shares on the NYSE for $20.00 due to Reg NMS. As a result, the same problem then arises that once the BATS trade is executed, the other 500 shares available may disappear before they can be purchased.

Again, the broker would route the 600 IBM share order to both exchanges simultaneously. The broker even has the flexibility to route the 500 share order to the NYSE before the 100 share order to BATS, if the broker reasonably believes this would achieve a lower fill price for the customer's order for IBM.

Example 3: On page 222–223, the example has a customer wishing to purchase 100,000 shares of P&G through a broker (Bank of America in this example). The customer is willing to pay up to $82.97. The broker first pings IEX looking to buy 100 shares, but then fails to send a larger order subsequently. In this example, Lewis suggests that a seller of 100,000 shares at $82.96 could have existed at IEX, which the broker missed. Instead the broker pings IEX with multiple 100 share orders, thus "goos[ing] up the price."

The flaw with this example is that the broker does not know that there is really a "seller waiting on it" for 100,000 shares. Furthermore, if the entire 100,000 share order had been sent, and only 1,000 was executed (since the example states that there are only 1,000 shares listed), the broker would have revealed the entire size of the order, thus dramatically "goosing" up the stock much more than the 100 share pings.

---

[30] Id.

[31] A trade-at rule requires brokers and dark pools to route trades to public exchanges, unless they can execute the trades at a meaningfully better price than available in a public market. It is unclear how the SEC would define a meaningfully better price.

PREPARED STATEMENT OF JEFFREY M. SOLOMON

Chief Executive Officer, Cowen and Company, LLC, and Cochair, Equity
Capital Formation Task Force

June 18, 2014

Over the past few years, there has been significant debate about the economic impact of High Frequency Trading (HFT) on the Equity Capital Markets in the United States. Much of this discussion focuses on the specific activities of these market participants and how the rise in their trading activity has introduced increased risk and volatility—even within the inner workings of equity market function. In other words, memories of the May 2010 ''Flash Crash'' are still fresh in the minds of market participants and fears of a repeat event are prevalent.

However, HFT, in and of itself, is not the root cause of increased market risk. Indeed, we would argue that the challenges surrounding HFT are actually a symptom of a more complex market structure that promotes and encourages potentially counterproductive trading behavior—behavior that reduces the availability of capital for smaller capitalization companies to expand their business and reduces liquidity for investors. As such, any debate about the pros and cons of HFT really needs to address the structure of the equity market that has given rise to its existence.

Today's market structure has evolved over the past decade and half as a result of several regulatory changes regarding trading increments, fair access and order routing changes just to name a few. To be clear, each of these changes was well intended and has had positive effects on market participants. Yet there are a significant number of market participants who have grown increasingly skeptical that the sum total of these changes has actually resulted in a market that is holistically better or worse.

Rather than debate that point, we are encouraging lawmakers and regulators to explore and implement modifications to the current market structure to further improve equity market function. In doing so, our aim should be to accomplish objectives that further enhance the capital markets in the United States, which are still the best in the world, but are increasingly under siege as other global marketplaces evolve. These goals should be clearly defined in their objectives, observable in their outcomes, and easily modified as additional data around market performance is gathered.

To be clear, if we remain stagnant in our approach to equity market structure in this country, we are increasingly putting our economic growth and private sector job creation at risk. Conversely, improvements to the equity market function will not only improve the market experience for all participants, but it will continue to foster the kind of economic activity that has been the hallmark of the American Experience since the outset of the Industrial Revolution. Later in this testimony, we will lay out specific observations around market structure that we strongly believe are inhibiting capital formation in industries that are vital to the continued economic growth of the United States.

In making assessments about market structure, we have encouraged regulators and legislators to be balanced and thoughtful in their approach, while attempting to implement change. With just about any market-developed convention, there are both positive and negative aspects to the presence of electronically driven trading firms that utilize algorithmic-based programs to identify profit opportunities and execute upon them. One such positive is that many market participants who engage in High Frequency Trading are able to generate profits at very thin trading spreads. This attribute has led to a significant reduction in transaction processing and execution costs which has translated into lower commissions paid by all market participants.

However, in the quest to accomplish this goal, we have created a highly fragmented marketplace that is quite hostile to the vital functions necessary to promote the capital formation that leads to private sector job growth. Not only has there been a substantial decline in small company IPOs over the past decade-and-a-half (transactions raising $60 million or less), but many small-cap public companies have also suffered from a lack of capital formation which has inhibited their ability to raise capital efficiently leading to limited job creation, innovation, and investment opportunities stemming from startups and small companies.

For this reason, a group of market participants representing a cross section of the startup and small-cap company ecosystem formed the Equity Capital Formation (ECF) Task Force to examine the challenges that America's startups and small-cap companies face in raising equity capital in the current public market environment and develop recommendations for policy makers that will help such companies gain greater access to the capital they need to grow their businesses, create new industries, provide increased competition to the markets, and ultimately create private sector job growth.

The attached report from the ECF Task Force, ''From the On-ramp to the Freeway: Refueling Job Creation and Growth by Reconnecting Investors With Small-Cap Companies'', was presented to the United States Treasury in November, 2013, and sets out two areas for consideration: (1) the implementation of a pilot program aimed at increasing liquidity in small-cap stocks by fostering a simpler, more orderly market structure for trading small-cap stocks and (2) the expansion of access to capital for small startups and micro-cap companies by completing the regulatory changes outlined in the JOBS Act relative to Regulation A+ and resolve conflicts with state laws. These recommendations are designed to enhance capital formation for small companies while balancing the needs of investor protection and preserving many of the important improvements made to the market structure to which we have become accustomed.

The United States' one-size-fits-all capital markets ecosystem makes capital formation for small-cap companies challenging. Today's market structure is marked by speed of execution, lower transaction costs and sub-penny increments, which favors liquid, large-cap stocks and inadvertently fosters illiquidity in small-cap stocks where the benefits of High Frequency Trading are less obvious. As we discuss in the attached report, for many small-cap investors, true price discovery and market depth are of greater importance than speed of execution. Indeed, the current market structure which favors speed over price discovery is highlighted as a key reason why institutional investors, who are the primary providers of capital for small companies, have remained on the sidelines—forgoing investment in this critical ecosystem because the risk of position illiquidity is too great.

A well-designed pilot trading program that allows for a true empirical test of the effects of wider spreads and limited increments in small-cap stocks will encourage fundamental buyers and sellers to meaningfully engage with each other, bringing the volume and depth necessary to enhance liquidity in the small-cap market. These proposed recommendations would extend to approximately 2 percent of the average daily market volume and would certainly be worth the upside of greatly expanded economic activity. Importantly, long-term market structure changes in the small-cap market will cause other market participants to adjust their trading practices and/or business models accordingly.

The health of the U.S. capital markets system is critical to driving private sector job growth and by extension, America's future prosperity. As stewards of this system and the public interest, policymakers and market participants have a duty to ensure that our markets remain fair and orderly, and that their benefits reach the largest number of Americans possible.

We have the opportunity to reexamine the current market structure as it relates to small companies and address some of the remaining barriers to accessing growth capital to further support the momentum generated by the success of the JOBS Act. We can support the growth of America's most promising private and public growth companies by allowing them to access the capital markets to fund their growth, create new industries and provide increased competition to the markets. We owe it to those seeking jobs and those small companies creating opportunities to try to adjust a small part of the market in order to bring job opportunities to those hard working individuals. And we can do it without sacrificing many of the benefits that many investors enjoy that were brought about by the advent of the current electronically driven market structure.

From the On-Ramp to the Freeway:

Refueling Job Creation and Growth by
Reconnecting Investors with Small-Cap Companies

Issued by the Equity Capital Formation Task Force
November 11, 2013

Presented to the U.S. Department of the Treasury

Table of Contents

Chart Index

I. Executive Summary

For generations, the U.S. capital markets have driven America's economic growth and generated millions of private sector jobs. The sustained success of this vital ecosystem stems largely from its ability – decade after decade – to provide an environment where today's most promising startup companies can develop into tomorrow's global leaders because investors are willing to provide them with the capital to do so. By the late 2000s, however, the barriers to accessing capital for many small **emerging growth companies** had grown significantly – leading to a downturn in the U.S. **initial public offering (IPO)** market and threatening the long-term health of the U.S. economy.

In 2012, Congress passed The Jumpstart Our Business Startups (JOBS Act) to address the IPO market downturn. The JOBS Act aimed to right-size the risks, costs and regulatory burdens that innovative startups face in becoming public companies. Importantly, it did so while preserving important investor protections implemented during the prior decade. Less than two years later, it is clear that the JOBS Act has re-energized interest in the public markets on the part of emerging growth companies. Almost immediately, it changed how small private companies approach the IPO process, and it has rekindled hope for companies that have been delayed or detoured from the public markets by a decade of adverse market conditions. More importantly, the JOBS Act has the potential to reignite interest in innovative technologies and revive the viability of business models that, without the prospect of an IPO, entrepreneurs and investors have deemed too capital-intensive to succeed. These are the very types of companies that can spawn entire new industries – spurring decades of private sector job creation and U.S. economic growth in the process.

Due to the momentum generated by the success of the JOBS Act, market participants and policy-makers now have the opportunity to address some of the remaining barriers in accessing growth capital faced not only by small private startups but also by many small capitalization companies that are already public. The process of undertaking an IPO and becoming a public company remains expensive. For the smallest companies, the five-year window for scaled compliance may close before the company has built sufficient revenue to absorb the cost of full public-company compliance. Similarly, publicly traded micro-caps may lack the financial resources to undertake the full registration process to raise smaller amounts of capital or even achieve listings on a national exchange. Both small startups and micro-caps benefit from greater access to capital, but they need a scaled down, more cost-efficient option than an IPO. Recognizing this need, Title IV of the JOBS Act aims to make Regulation A more accessible to startups. However, policy-makers have yet to complete a number of critical mandates in Title IV, and must make small amendments to the Securities Act of 1933 to resolve remaining conflicts between new JOBS Act provisions and state laws. As long as these issues remain unresolved, this otherwise low-cost and viable alternative tool for capital formation will remain unavailable to promising startups and micro-cap companies.

Recommendation #1:

Expand access to capital for small startups and micro-caps by completing the JOBS Act's mandates regarding Regulation A and resolving conflicts with state laws.

1.1   Implement Title IV of the JOBS Act immediately so that Regulation A+ becomes a viable option for small startup and micro-cap capital formation.

1.2.   Amend Section 18(b)(4)(D) of the Securities Act to permit preemption of state securities laws for:

  (a)   all securities offered pursuant to Regulation A or Regulation A+; or

  (b)   securities sold pursuant to Regulation A or Regulation A+ provided such securities are offered or sold through a registered broker dealer.

1.3.   Alternatively or in addition thereto, define "qualified purchaser" under Section 18(b)(4)(D) in a manner that would enable small business issuers to rely on preemption of state securities laws for Regulation A or Regulation A+ purposes.

42

1.4. Amend Section 18(b)(4) to clarify that secondary sales of Regulation A and Regulation A+ securities are similarly preempted from state securities laws.

Furthermore, policy-makers also have the opportunity to mitigate some of the challenges to post-IPO capital formation that emerging growth companies and other **small-cap** companies face. Chief among these challenges is an illiquid trading market for small-cap stocks. The rise of electronic trading and the regulations governing order handling, pricing and execution that followed have created a new market structure for equities trading marked by speed of execution and lower transaction costs. While these new dynamics work well in highly liquid, large cap stocks, they actually foster opacity and illiquidity in the small-cap market. This illiquidity makes it more costly and difficult for investors to invest, trade and make markets in small-cap stocks. Under these conditions, many **institutional investors** have not scaled their allocations to strategies that invest in small capitalization stocks. This development is significant because domestic equity small-cap mutual funds, which represent a major segment of institutional investors, hold $409 billion assets[1] - much of it on behalf of U.S. households. Generally speaking, less institutional participation in the small-cap market leads to less trading volume and liquidity for most small-cap stocks, as well as less equity capital to provide growth. Absent this liquidity, small-cap companies struggle to attract the type of long-term investors that enable them to continue to raise the equity capital they need to sustain job creation and growth after their IPOs. The resultant lack of liquidity also harms the largely **individual investor** base that currently holds the majority of ownership in many small-cap stocks by muting the price appreciation they hope to capture through long-term investment. Again, this price appreciation cannot happen unless institutions accumulate **positions** and provide liquidity in these stocks. Given these dynamics, the Equity Capital Formation Task Force believes that the current market structure is not adequately serving the needs of small-cap companies as it relates to their ability to access capital, or the needs of the investors who would benefit from a more liquid market in which to buy and sell small-cap stocks. For this reason, the task force recommends developing new "rules of the road" for simplifying the trading of small-cap stocks (which the task force calls Small-cap Trading Rules, or STaR,) and testing their effects via a carefully considered, well-designed pilot trading program.

Recommendation #2:

Encourage increased liquidity in small-cap stocks by fostering a simpler, more orderly market structure for small-cap companies and investors.

2.1. The national exchanges should conduct a pilot trading program, overseen by the SEC, in which select small-cap companies trade under new Small-Cap Trading Rules (STaR). Under STaR:

    2.1.1 Participating companies will have market capitalizations below $750 million.

    2.1.2 Participating companies should be quoted in minimum price increments of $0.05 and trade only at the bid, the offer or the mid-point between the two.

2.2 The SEC and the national exchanges should begin the process of designing and implementing the STaR pilot as soon as is feasible.

2.3. The STaR pilot design must include a clear methodology for collecting and analyzing data regarding STaR's effects on small-cap trading. Metrics should include (a) relative level of trading liquidity, (b) changes in institutional ownership, and (c) rate of equity capital issuance.

2.4. The STaR pilot must run long enough to provide a true empirical test of STaR's effects on the small-cap market.

2.5 At the STaR pilot's conclusion, the SEC must use the empirical data generated by the pilot to

---

[1] Morningstar. As of June 2013. "Small-cap" includes small value, small blend, small growth funds.

evaluate whether Small-Cap Trading Rules should apply to small-cap trading on a permanent basis.

The Equity Capital Formation Task Force developed the action steps above to be highly specific, targeted and limited in application only to startups and small-cap companies. In all, the latter represents only 2 percent of trading volume on U.S. equities exchanges.[2]

The health of the U.S. capital markets system is essential to driving critical private sector job growth and by extension, America's future prosperity. As stewards of this system and the public interest, policy-makers have a responsibility to ensure that our markets remain fair and orderly, and that their benefits reach the largest number of Americans possible. The task force believes that by taking these action steps now, policy-makers can help refuel capital formation for America's most promising private and public growth companies.

"We should never forget why there is a market. We seem to forget that in all the discussion about market structure." — Oyvind G. Schanke, Norges Bank Investment Management[3]

---

[2] *Bloomberg*

[3] *http://dealbook.nytimes.com/2013/10/20/wealth-fund-cautions-against-costs-exacted-by-high-speed-trading/?_r=0*

II. Statement of Purpose

Comprising professionals from across America's startup and small-capitalization company ecosystems, the Equity Capital Formation (ECF) Task Force formed in June 2013 to 1) examine the challenges that America's startups and small-cap companies face in raising equity capital in the current public market environment, and 2) develop recommendations for policy-makers that will help such companies gain greater access to the capital they need to grow their businesses and generate private sector job growth. The task force's efforts have been informed by discussions flowing from The Securities and Exchange Commission's Decimalization Roundtable (February 2013), which examined the impacts of decimalized pricing of securities on IPOs, trading, and liquidity for small and middle capitalization companies; and from the Capital Access Innovation Summit convened by the Treasury Department and the Small Business Administration in June 2013, which focused on the impact of the JOBS Act of 2012 on capital formation for emerging growth companies and what additional measures might benefit this process. This report outlines the Equity Capital Formation Task Force's findings and recommendations.

45

III. Introduction

For generations, the U.S. capital markets have been the envy of the world by driving America's economic growth and generating millions of private sector jobs. The sustained success of this system stems largely from its ability – decade after decade – to develop today's most promising startups into tomorrow's global leaders. It does so by providing those companies with efficient access to the public capital they need to grow and create jobs, and by enabling a wide array of investors to participate directly in that growth through fair and orderly markets. According to the Kauffman Foundation, companies that go public increase their employment levels by approximately 45 percent after their **initial public offerings (IPOs)**. More significantly, for small company IPOs, that number more than triples to 156 percent.[4]

By the late 2000s, however, the challenges that innovative startups faced in getting to the public markets, and in realizing the benefits of doing so, had grown significantly. As a result, the number of yearly IPOs dropped significantly between 1996 and 2011, as did the number of listed companies on national exchanges in the U.S. These developments not only robbed the U.S. economy of a generation of leading companies, but led to less capital formation, and, in turn, less job creation. In fact, the U.S. economy may have created 1.87 million[5] fewer private sector jobs over this time period as a result.

Chart A: Total Equity Listings

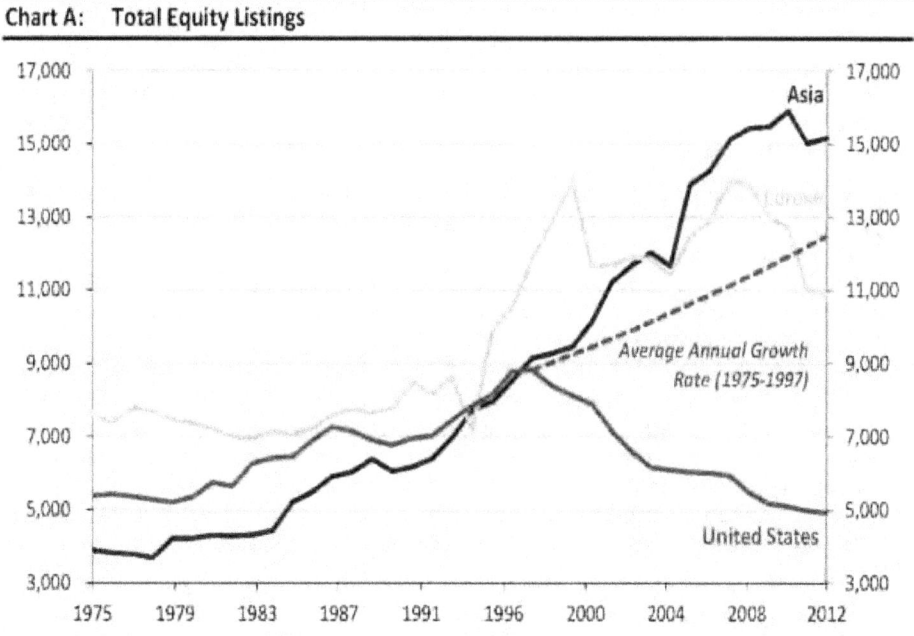

Source: Source: Weild, David and Kim, Edward. IssuWorks. Voss, Jason. CFA Institute.

> The U.S. economy may have created 1.87 million fewer private sector jobs as a result of the IPO market downturn.

---

[4] Post-IPO Employment and Revenue Growth for U.S. IPOs, June 1996-2010. (May 2012)

[5] Ritter, Jay R. "Re-energizing the IPO Market." (December 2012)

IV. The Road to the Public Markets

A. The JOBS Act Reopens the On-Ramp

In early 2012, lawmakers took action to address the downturn in the IPO market. Working in a bipartisan manner, Congress passed the Jumpstart Our Business Startups (JOBS) Act, which President Obama signed into law in April 2012. The JOBS Act incorporates a number of innovative measures aimed at reducing the burdens and costs that promising startups faced on the path to the public markets. Most importantly, it applied the principle – already in place for a select group of small companies – that regulatory burdens should be commensurate with a company's size, and increase as it matures, to a new category of companies called **emerging growth companies** (EGCs). This new scaled compliance regime aimed to lower the time and cost burdens that EGCs face in preparing to become public companies, and to reduce the risks associated with initiating the IPO process. It also aimed to accomplish these objectives while preserving important investor protections implemented over the prior decade.

B. A Surge of Traffic

Less than two years later, it is clear that the JOBS Act has re-energized interest in the public markets on the part of emerging growth companies. Since the law's enactment, more than 200 companies have registered with the SEC as emerging growth companies. That represents 79 percent of all companies who have filed to go public over this time.[6] As of October 25, 2013, there were 63 companies in registration for an IPO – including 48 registered as EGCs. Additionally, Renaissance Capital's Private Company Watchlist estimates that there are 225 IPOs currently in confidential registration or are likely to register soon.[7] The law has also rekindled hope for companies that have been delayed or detoured from the public markets by a decade of adverse market conditions.

> *79% of companies that have filed to go public since the JOBS Act have registered as EGCs.*

The JOBS Act has not only renewed interest in IPOs, but has also transformed how startups approach the IPO process while continuing their growth. First, thanks to scaled compliance with provisions such as SOX 404(b), EGCs can focus their capital on growing their companies and creating jobs. Meanwhile, management can focus its attention on strategy, operations and successful execution of company business plans. Second, the law's "test the waters" provision enables management to build relationships with institutions and research analysts, get feedback on the company's strategy, and gauge interest from investors before committing to an offering. After receiving valuable market feedback from public company investors, if company management or its board of directors believes the company isn't ready, the company can pull back without penalty, embarrassment or significant cost outlay. Finally, the law's confidential filing provision enables EGCs to begin the IPO filing process while still retaining the ability to protect intellectual property and other valuable strategic assets from competitors. In the year after the JOBS Act was signed, 63 percent of companies that registered with the SEC as EGCs used the confidential filling provision.[8]

C. Increased IPO Flow

While the JOBS Act immediately re-energized interest by startups in going public, its impact on the actual number of IPOs has been – as many experts expected – more steady than explosive. As of October 25, 2013, 154 companies had gone public[9], versus 121 in all of 2012.[10] Similarly, through the same period, 2013

---

[6] *Dealogic and Renaissance Capital as of October 25, 2013.*

[7] *Ibid.*

[8] *"The JOBS Act One Year Later: A Review of the New IPO Playbook." Latham & Watkins April 2013.*

[9] *As of 10/25/2013.*

[10] *Dealogic.*

produced 53 micro-cap (less than $250 million market cap) IPOs, versus 32 in all of 2012. In terms of percentage of all IPOs, companies with less than $250 million market cap have constituted 34 percent of IPOs so far in 2013 – up from 26 percent in 2012.[11]

The fact that the JOBS Act has helped to spur more IPOs has benefitted EGCs and investors alike. Through the third quarter of 2013, EGCs had raised a total $26.2 billion in equity capital – capital that can be used to advance product development, scale-up production capacity, build out marketing and distribution capabilities, and – most importantly – hire new employees. In addition, the value accrued to public market investors in these IPOs has been significant. The average EGC IPO currently trades at 64 percent above its initial offering price, compared to 30 percent for non-EGCs.[12]

In addition to its immediate impact on the IPO space, the JOBS Act has the potential to deliver even greater benefits to startups, investors and the American public in the future. By restoring the IPO as a credible option for EGCs and their investors to raise capital to stay independent, the JOBS Act can reignite interest in game-changing technologies and revive the viability of business models that, without the prospect of an IPO, entrepreneurs and investors have deemed too capital-intensive to succeed. These are the very types of companies that can spawn entire new industries – providing decades of job creation and U.S. economic growth in the process. However, such outcomes are far from guaranteed, due to some difficult conditions that persist beyond the IPO "on-ramp" and out on the public market.

Chart B:	JOBS Act Impact – the Stats
On the On-Ramp:	63 companies currently in registration with the SEC.[13]
Estimated Backlog:	225 estimated companies in confidential registration for an IPO or deemed close to registering for an IPO per Renaissance Capital's Private Company Watchlist.
Sparked Interest:	More than 200 companies have registered with the SEC as emerging growth companies since the JOBS Act – representing 79% of all companies who have filed to go public over this time.[14]
IPO Confidential:	One year post-JOBS Act, 63% of companies that registered with the SEC as EGCs used the confidential filing provision.[15]
Trending Up:	Companies with less than $250 million market caps have constituted 34% of IPOs so far in 2013 — up from 26% in 2012.[16]
Dollars Raised:	$28.5 billion in proceeds from EGC companies.[17]
Aftermarket Performance:	EGC IPOs are up average of 64.2% offer/current versus 30.4% for the non-EGC IPOs in the comparable period.[18]

[11] Ibid.

[13] Bloomberg; Dealogic.

[12] Dealogic and Renaissance Capital as of October 25, 2013.

[14] Ibid.

[14] "The JOBS Act One Year Later: A Review of the New IPO Playbook." Latham & Watkins April 2013.

[18] Dealogic.

[17] Ibid.

[18] Bloomberg; Dealogic.

Chart C: JOBS Act Impact — the Stories

Bluebird Bio
(NASDAQ:BLUE)

Founded 1992 / IPO 2013

Focus: Innovative gene therapies for severe genetic and orphan diseases.

Nick Leschly, *CEO:*
"Our IPO has enabled us to plan and hire against a more aggressive strategic plan. Under the JOBS Act, the ability to file confidentially was incredibly important because it enabled us to keep more strategic options on the table, which is important in the face of the uncertainty involved with an IPO. In addition, the ability to 'test the waters' provided us visibility into our potential investor base, which allowed us to make more informed decisions about our strategic direction."

LifeLock
(NYSE:LOCK)

Founded 2005 / IPO 2012

Focus: Leading provider of proactive identity theft protection services for consumers and identity risk assessment and fraud protection services for enterprises.

Todd Davis, *CEO:*
"LifeLock's decision to go public and raise the capital needed to invest in the technology and people we need to protect Americans from rapidly-evolving threats of identity theft was one of our most important strategic decisions of the past few years. While the process was appropriately rigorous, the greater access to resources to re-invest in our business made it a good choice. We should do whatever we can to streamline the process and make the option more attractive and easier for companies in the future."

Portola
(NASDAQ:PTLA)

Founded 2003 / IPO 2013

Focus: Fighting blood clots and bleeding disorders.

Mardi Dier, *CFO:*
"Prior to our IPO, we were operating with a thin staff due to the uncertain financing environment. Since then, we have increased our employee base by 20 percent and we expect to grow even more. The 'testing the waters' provision of the JOBS Act gave us extra time with investors to tell our story, and gave investors extra time to do their homework on us. I think that was a key to our IPO's success."

Applied Optoelectronics
(NASDAQ:AAOI)

Founded 1997 / IPO 2013

Focus: Advanced optical devices, packaged optical components, optical subsystems, laser transmitters, and fiber optic transceivers.

James Dunn, *CFO:*
"With the capital provided by the IPO, we plan to add two production lines in the U.S. With that expansion, we expect to drive revenue and increase overall production, which will ultimately lead to additional jobs being created in the U.S. – specifically in fostering R&D. Our biggest challenge will be to understand that this is a long-term effort, and that the IPO is only the beginning of that effort."

V. Roadblocks for Startups and EGCs Remain

A. Small Startups Need More Options for Capital Formation

Amidst the IPO market downturn of the 2000s, the market segment representing IPOs under $50 million in proceeds experienced the steepest decline. Formerly accounting for 80 percent of yearly IPOs[19], under-$50 million IPOs fell to 8 percent since 2012.[20] While this segment has witnessed a modest rebound in the wake of the JOBS Act, this task force believes that small startups need more options for accessing public capital than just an IPO.

Even with the On-Ramp provisions, the process of undertaking an IPO and becoming a public company remains expensive. For the smallest companies, the five-year window for scaled compliance may close before the company has built sufficient revenue to meet the costs of full public company compliance. Similarly, small private companies as well as publicly traded micro-caps may lack the financial resources to undertake the full registration process to raise smaller amounts of capital or achieve listing on a national exchange. Such companies still need capital to continue product development, build their marketing and distribution capabilities and hire new employees – just not on the scale to justify the extra levels of cost and risk that a small IPO or follow-on offering would incur. However, due to their size and their risk profiles, raising capital from private networks or through debt financing remains difficult for small startups. For this reason, promising small companies need a viable option between these conventional methods and an IPO to raise the capital they need to grow.

WHO NEEDS REGULATION A+?

Regulation A+ could provide small private companies and micro-cap companies with a scaled, cost-efficient option for raising public capital. Small biotechnology companies provide a poignant example: Many have market caps in excess of $250 million (because investors value these companies based on the present value of future potential earnings), but can generate very little revenue deep into their lives as public companies. This is because their core products can remain in the research, development and testing phases for a decade or more. These expensive processes, coupled with daily operating expenses and public company regulatory compliance costs, can significantly limit the resources these companies can deploy for hiring, product development and growth. Providing these companies with more cost-efficient options for raising capital could mean the difference between whether or not a significant medical breakthrough ultimately reaches the hands of doctors and patients.

Title IV of the JOBS Act[21] aimed to provide a lower cost alternative to an IPO by raising the offering limits for "small public offerings" under Regulation A and delegating authority to the SEC to resolve other issues that have limited the use of Regulation A prior to the JOBS Act. These issues include the costs of disclosure and compliance obligations for small companies under Regulation A, relative to the limited offering size, and the qualification requirements under state securities laws.[22]

---

[19] Represents IPOs from 1991 to 1997, prior to electronic-order-book market. Source: Weild, David, with E. Kim and L. Newport. Grant Thornton, "The Trouble with Small Tick Sizes." (September 2012)

[20] Dealogic.

[21] Jumpstart Our Business Startups Act, Pub. L. No. 112-106, Title IV (2012)

[22] Rutheford B. Campbell, Jr., Regulation A: small Business' Search for 'A Moderate Capital', 31 Del. J. Corp. L. (2006); Rutheford B. Campbell, Jr. Regulation A and the JOBS Act: A Failure To Resuscitate, (2012) [hereinafter, "Campbell, A Failure to Resuscitate"].

So far, Title IV has not achieved the desired result, as Regulation A remains virtually unused.[23] The reasons for this are two-fold: 1) The SEC has not yet issued the rules mandated in Title IV, and 2) Title IV does not adequately address one of the key barriers limiting the appeal and utility of Regulation A: preemption of state securities laws. As long as these issues remain unresolved, this otherwise low-cost and viable alternative tool for capital formation will remain unavailable to promising young startups.

"Without legislation to supplement the JOBS Act, Emerging Growth Companies could be left to die on the vine, in reach of vital public capital but unable to fully access it." —Kenneth Moch, CEO, Chimerix, Inc.

---

[23] Ibid.

B. Post-IPO, Small-Caps and Investors Need Liquidity for Capital Formation

In the style of the landmark Securities Act of 1933, the JOBS Act focuses on the process by which a company enters the public markets. However, while an IPO may be the most important step in an emerging growth company's development, it is only Day One of that company's life in the public market. Today, many small-cap companies are finding life there extremely difficult – not necessarily because of their operating performance, but rather due to a number of challenges afflicting the **aftermarket** support system on which newly public companies depend for follow-on capital raises necessary for future growth.

Chief among these challenges is an illiquid trading market for small-cap stocks. In its simplest sense, a liquid market is one in which buyers and sellers openly display their price and volume trading expectations in order to facilitate the execution of a stock trade. This type of "efficient" market balances the broad-based needs of issuers, **individual investors** and their agents. By attracting the broadest base of investors, companies achieve a level of liquidity that is commensurate with their size. Absent a liquid market, small-cap companies cannot attract long-term **institutional investors**, including those that administer mutual funds and pension funds, who are necessary to provide the growth capital required by these companies to fund their post-IPO growth needs. Long-term investors eschew illiquid markets because they are affected by what is commonly referred to as an "illiquidity tax," under which the investor materially moves the price of a stock up when they accumulate a **position** in it, and down when they sell that position. The "illiquidity tax" makes it uneconomical for many long-term institutional investors to invest in small-cap stocks relative to larger stocks with more **trading liquidity**.

For this reason, investors generally value liquid stocks more highly than illiquid stocks. That's important because a company's market valuation plays a key role in determining how much equity capital the company can raise, and at what cost, in future financing events over its lifetime. Companies with liquid stocks that have demonstrated they can achieve a fully-valued[24] stock price can more easily issue follow-on offerings, or use their stock as currency to fund acquisitions, compensate employees and compete for talent. By contrast, those public companies with a poor trading liquidity profile are sometimes unable to raise additional capital through the public markets, or can only do so at a higher cost of capital.[25] This dynamic can constrain their growth and, in many cases, can defeat the purpose of going public in the first place.

Unfortunately, over the past decade and a half, hundreds of companies have learned this lesson the hard way. As a result, secondary market trading liquidity in the small-cap market has become a serious consideration for any company when it weighs the risks and costs of going public versus other financing alternatives or exit strategies. As long as the view from the IPO "on-ramp" suggests that the prospect of taking on all of the additional costs and risks of going public, but struggling to capture the benefits, many startup founders, managers and investors will continue to think twice about choosing to finance their growth via the public market.

---

[24] Keating, Tim. Keating Investments, "Analyzing the Analysts: A Survey of the State of Wall Street Equity Research 10 Years after the Global Settlement." (January 2013). Based on price-to-sales ratio.

[25] Ibid.

VI. Recommendations

As discussed in prior sections, the success of the JOBS Act has created an opportunity for market participants and policy-makers to remove additional barriers to capital formation for private startups, EGCs and small-cap companies. In order to improve access to capital for additional small startups and micro-caps, we must give these companies more cost-effective options for accessing investor capital. In order to move more promising small companies from the "on-ramp" to the "freeway," as well as improve capital formation for liquidity-challenged small-caps, we will need to increase trading liquidity for small-cap companies and the investors who want to invest in them. Doing so will require action by policy-makers and market participants on two fronts:

Improved Access to Capital: Completing the On-Ramp for Promising Small Companies

While the JOBS Act has re-opened the on-ramp to the public markets for many promising startups, small companies for which an IPO may not be cost effective remain in need of alternative options for accessing public capital. Title IV of the JOBS Act recognizes this need by calling for modifications to Regulation A. However, those modifications have not yet been made – leaving many promising small startups and micro-cap companies with the same capital formation challenges they faced prior to the JOBS Act.

Recommendation #1:

Expand access to capital for small startups and micro-caps by completing the JOBS Act's mandates regarding Regulation A and resolving conflicts with state laws.

Market Structure: Improving Capital Flow on the Freeway

The current market structure is not serving the needs of small-cap companies or the investors who wish to buy and sell their stocks. Specifically, quote increments of $0.01 and the ability to trade in between pennies at fractions of one cent make it difficult for fundamental investors to find adequate trading liquidity in which they can accumulate or exit meaningful investment positions in small-cap stocks. As a result, many institutional investors – including those who invest an estimated $409 billion in small-cap U.S. equities through mutual funds[26] – have found it more difficult to invest in small-caps. The resulting lack of liquidity makes it even more difficult for these companies to raise capital beyond their IPOs to fund hiring, product development and expansion of their marketing and distribution capabilities.

Recommendation #2:

Encourage increased liquidity in small-cap stocks by fostering a simpler, more orderly market structure for small-cap companies and investors.

These challenges and recommendations are examined in depth in the following pages.

---

[26] Morningstar. As of June 2013. "Small-cap" includes small value, small blend, small growth funds.

A. Improved Access to Capital: Completing the On-Ramp for Promising Small Companies

Recommendation #1:

Expand access to capital for small startups and micro-caps by completing the JOBS Act's mandates regarding Regulation A and resolving conflicts with state laws.

Prior to the JOBS Act, small companies looking for a more cost-efficient option for raising investor capital than an IPO were limited to private placements, a 506(c) offering under Regulation D, or an offering under Regulation A. By design, each option has its limits. In the first two cases, the trading in the resulting security is restricted, and as such, provides less liquidity to investors (the implications of which are described on page 11.) By contrast, a Regulation A offering results in a security that can be traded publicly, but Regulation A has gone virtually unused by startups and micro-caps.

Regulation A provides an exemption for offerings up to only $5 million for issuers who are not subject to the reporting requirements of section 13 or 15(d) of the Securities Exchange Act of 1934 (the "Exchange Act") immediately prior to the offering.[27] The Regulation A exemption is subject to the filing of a Form 1-A with specified disclosure requirements, allows widespread solicitation, does not require purchaser qualifications and allows unlimited resale of securities purchased pursuant to Regulation A. The reasons for the relative non-usage of Regulation A include the costs of disclosure and compliance obligations relative to the limited offering size (notwithstanding that the disclosure requirements are less than those required by Form S-1) and the often costly and burdensome qualification requirements under state securities laws.[28]

Title IV of the JOBS Act delegates to the SEC the authority to enact regulations to address the issues that have effectively rendered Regulation A non-viable as an alternative for efficient, broad-based capital formation for small businesses. Specifically, Title IV added a new section 3(b)(2) to Section 3(b) of the Securities Act of 1933 (the "Securities Act"), which requires the SEC to enact a new regulation to exempt offerings of up to $50 million in any 12-month period from registration. Additionally, section 3(b)(2) requires that:

(a) such exemption be conditioned upon an issuer filing annual audited financial statements.[29]
(b) the securities shall not be restricted securities;
(c) that section 12(a)(2) civil liabilities will apply;
(d) the securities may be offered and sold publicly; and
(e) the issuer may solicit interest in the offering prior to the filing of any offering, on such terms and conditions that the SEC may prescribe in the public interest or for the protection of investors.[30]

Further, new section 3(b)(2) provides that the SEC may enact other requirements it deems necessary in the public interest and for protection of investors, which may include requiring investors to file an offering statement, as well as ongoing periodic disclosures, with the SEC and prohibiting "bad actors" from availing themselves of the new exemption.[31] Last, and perhaps most significantly, Title IV amends Section 18(b)(4) of the Securities Act to exempt offerings made pursuant to new section 3(b)(2), provided the securities are offered and sold on a national exchange or offered or sold to a qualified purchaser, as defined by the SEC. In

---

[27] *Issuers must also be U.S. or Canadian issuers and may not be: a development stage company with no specific business plan or purpose or has indicated plan is to merge with unidentified company, an investment company, an entity issuing fractional undivided interests in oil or gas rights or similar interests in other mineral rights or disqualified under section 262. Regulation A, 17 C.F.R. §§ 230.251-.263 (2012).*

[28] *Rutheford B. Campbell, Jr., Regulation A: Small Business' Search for 'A Moderate Capital', 31 Del. J. Corp. L. (2006); Rutheford B. Campbell, Jr., Regulation A and the JOBS Act: A Failure To Resuscitate, (2012) (hereinafter, "Campbell, A Failure to Resuscitate").*

[29] *Currently under Regulation A, issuers are required to provide financial statements but such financial statements need not be audited.*

[30] *15 U.S.C. 5 77(b) (2012).*

[31] *Ibid.*

other words, state securities laws would be preempted for offerings made under section 3(b)(2) as those securities would be "covered securities", but only if such securities are traded on a national exchange or are offered or sold to a qualified purchaser.

However, Title IV does not appear to have had, and likely will not have, any measurable impact on the use of Regulation A as a means for small businesses to access capital. The reasons for the relative non-usage of Regulation A include the costs of disclosure and compliance obligations relative to the limited offering size (notwithstanding that the disclosure requirements are less than those required by Form S-1) and the often costly and burdensome qualification requirements under state securities laws.

Absent the enactment of the mandatory or discretionary provisions of Title IV, issuers are limited to current Regulation A, which has been relatively unused. Second, absent clarification or amendment, one of the barriers to more widespread appeal and utility of Regulation A, namely preemption of state securities laws, remains a significant obstacle under Title IV. Specifically, although Title IV provides that state securities laws will be preempted for section 3(b)(2) offerings, this preemption is predicated on the securities being traded on a national exchange or offered or sold to a qualified purchaser. With respect to the former, most small businesses are not likely to have their securities traded on a national exchange and, if required to do so, would incur additional burdensome compliance costs associated therewith. With respect to the latter, until the term "qualified purchaser" is defined, small business issuers are unable to rely on that provision for preemption purposes. Accordingly, section 18(b)(4)(D) in its current form does not adequately resolve the issue of preemption of state securities laws. It would seem incongruous to deem securities sold through Regulation A+ to be freely tradable at the federal level but to remain restricted at the state level, yet that remains the case. Absent resolution of the preemption issue, small business issuers will need to analyze and comply with the securities laws of the various and multiple jurisdictions in which it may offer or sell securities under Regulation A, as amended under Title IV or otherwise. In addition to the significant costs associated with such compliance, it is not clear that compliance with an applicable exemption under state securities laws would permit issuers to take advantage of some of the intended benefits of Title IV and section 3(b)(2), including "testing the waters" or general solicitation provisions of section 3(b)(2).

Detailed Recommendations:

1.1 Implement Title IV of the JOBS Act immediately so that Regulation A+ becomes a viable option for small startup and micro-cap capital formation.

1.2 Amend Section 18(b)(4)(D) of the Securities Act to permit preemption of state securities laws for:

(a) all securities offered pursuant to Regulation A or Regulation A+; or

(b) securities sold pursuant to Regulation A or Regulation A+ provided such securities are offered or sold through a registered broker dealer.

1.3 Alternatively or in addition thereto, define "qualified purchaser" under Section 18(b)(4)(D) in a manner that would enable small business issuers to rely on preemption of state securities laws for Regulation A or Regulation A+ purposes.

1.4 Amend Section 18(b)(4) to clarify that secondary sales of Regulation A and Regulation A+ securities are similarly preempted from state securities laws.

Analysis:

Making "Regulation A+" a reality for small startups and micro-caps will provide these companies with a number of critical benefits in their efforts to raise capital to grow and create jobs in the private sector. It will provide them with a lower cost, less burdensome process for raising public capital – a scaled registration, so to speak. Although the process involves less rigor than a full registration, there is a level of due diligence and disclosure involved in a Regulation A+ offering that mitigates some of that risk for potential investors. In addition, this process provides early exposure and relationship-building opportunities for offering companies with an investor pool that trades in micro-cap stocks. Similarly, a full Regulation A+ process enables startups and micro-caps to use important JOBS Act options such as "test the waters" and "general solicitation." Going forward, the Regulation A+ process results in a security that can be traded publicly, which provides more trading liquidity than other options such as a private placement or 506(c) offering. Finally, the entire process provides an invaluable primer for the full registration process, should a company's growth make a follow-on issue or listing on a national exchange viable options.

The foregoing recommendations, coupled with implementation of ongoing periodic disclosure requirements which are reasonable in scope, balance investor protection concerns with regulatory and compliance costs, and will provide small businesses with a truly viable alternative for efficient, broad-based capital formation.

B. Market Structure: Improving Capital Flow on the Freeway

Recommendation #2:

Encourage increased liquidity in small-cap stocks by fostering a simpler, more orderly market structure for small-cap companies and investors.

Quite a few market observers have chronicled the changes that have occurred in the U.S. equities markets since the mid-1990s. Many have reached a similar conclusion: The rise of electronic trading and the regulations governing order handling, pricing and execution that followed have created a new market structure for equities trading marked by faster execution speeds and lower transaction costs. By 2010, it was estimated that electronic trading accounted for more than 70 percent of equity trades taking place in the U.S.[82] These developments have produced a new generation of algorithm-based trading strategies that focus on high-volume, **large-cap** stocks and often prioritize speed of execution over price of execution.

Within this new market structure, the economics of large-cap trading remain relatively healthy, as the combination of low transaction costs, low trading commissions and high volume provides sufficient incentive for **market makers** to create active markets for these stocks. For this reason, the ECF Task Force is *not recommending* changes to trading practices for large-cap stocks. However, while narrower spreads and lower transaction costs have benefitted many investors, they are not the only meaningful metrics for measuring the health of the overall market ecosystem. Nor do they come without tradeoffs and costs of their own. So far, analysis on the part of many academics and market observers overwhelmingly suggests that these costs are being borne disproportionately by small-cap companies and **fundamentals**-based investors — both institutional and individual — who want to buy, sell or hold small-cap stocks as part of a long-term investment strategy.

From the small company perspective, the new market economics have put significant strain on the aftermarket support system for small-cap stocks. This effect goes beyond merely suppressing the number of IPOs over the last decade and a half. It's a structural issue, as the entire support system of small investment banks, institutional sales desks, market makers and research analysts has been decimated by the new market economics. With less support for life after their IPOs, fewer startups may see the public markets as offering the best option in their quest to evolve into large, enduring institutions. In short, they may turn away from the IPO "on-ramp" – whether it's "open" or not.

Chart D: Small-Cap Companies and Capital Formation

	Before 1997	After 2001	% change
Tick sizes	$0.25 per share	$0.01 per share	-96%
Investment banks (acting as a bookrunner)	167 (1994)	39 (2006)	-77%
Small company IPOs	2,990 (1991–1997)	233 (2001–2007)	-92%

Source: Weild, David, with E. Kim and L. Newport. Grant Thornton, "The Trouble with Small Tick Sizes," (September 2012)

For institutional investors, the new market structure has made it more difficult and costly to trade, invest in and make markets in small-cap stocks. That's because many of the new trading strategies – driven by faster execution speeds, lower transaction costs and sub-penny increments – that have proved so effective in large-cap trading actually foster opacity and illiquidity in small-cap trading. The following provides an example of this dynamic at work:

---

[82] Themis Trading http://blog.themistrading.com/to-be-honest/

Suppose an institution were to post an offer to sell a lot of 1,000 shares of a small-cap stock at the price of $5.00. Under the current trading regime, another market participant can quickly "step in front" of that order at virtually no cost by offering to sell shares in the same company at a price that can be as little as 1/10 of a penny lower than the $5.00 ask. Moreover, the trader who is "stepping in front" can execute the trade off-exchange with an incoming order from one of his customers, thereby precluding the original price setter from having its original advertised trade executed.

> "The U.S. market has gone through a lot of changes and has become quite complicated — and this complexity of the market creates a lot of challenges for a large investor like us." — Oyvind G. Schanke, Norges Bank Investment Management, which holds $110 billion in U.S. stocks.[33]

To defend against the scenario above, many institutional investors and traders now break their large blocks into many series of smaller lots in order to appear to the market as small retail orders. This practice adds extra time and costs to the process of accumulating or exiting significant positions in small-cap stocks. In fact, one estimate puts the costs to the overall market of "stepping in front" of orders at five to 10 times that of any other cost.[34] Worse, this practice reduces liquidity in the market for these stocks. In fact, the combination of low liquidity and higher risk in the form of single-stock volatility has prompted many institutions to underinvest in the small-cap market. This is significant for two reasons:

- First, research points to a positive correlation between higher levels of institutional ownership and more liquidity and higher company valuations.[35] On the other hand, lower levels of institutional ownership correlate to less liquidity and lower valuations. As outlined on page 11, this lack of liquidity can lead to lower valuations and constrain a company's ability to raise capital. In turn, this makes it more difficult to hire more employees, invest in research and development, and increase the overall scale and scope of its enterprise. In this sense, small companies once again bear the brunt of the new market structure's cost.

- Second, the costs and effects of small-cap market trading dynamics on institutional investment strategies are not limited to the institutions themselves. That's because individual investors are increasingly participating in the equities markets through mutual funds [see Chart F], most of which are managed by insitutions. For many Americans, mutual funds are the only choices offered through their employer-provided retirement plans. In fact, according to a recent survey by the ICI, 93 percent of mutual fund owners invest in such funds in order to build their retirement funds.[36] Domestic equity small-cap mutual funds now hold $409 billion in assets[37] – much of it on behalf of U.S. households. For these reasons, the traditional distinction between institutional and individual investors – and what market dynamics benefit one or the other – has become increasingly difficult to draw clearly. What is clear is that institutional participation in the small-cap market affects millions of individual investors who access the equities market through no other investment vehicle. Increasing this participation on the part of individual investors could connect billions of additional investment dollars from average Americans with the emerging growth companies that need those dollars most for capital expansion – and that offer the greatest potential for long-term growth.

[33] http://dealbook.nytimes.com/2013/10/20/wealth-fund-cautions-against-costs-exacted-by-high-speed-trading/?_r=0

[34] Ibid.

[35] Keating, Tim. Keating Investments. "Analyzing the Analysts: A Survey of the State of Wall Street Equity Research 10 Years after the Global Settlement." (January 2013).

[36] Investment Company Institute. 2013

[37] Morningstar. As of June 2013. "Small-cap" includes small value, small blend, small growth funds.

Chart E: Mutual Funds Snapshot

U.S. Mutual Fund Assets:	$13 trillion at year-end 2012[38]
Percentage of Mutual Funds Assets Owned by Households:	89%[39]
Percentage of Mutual Funds in Equities:	45%[40]
Assets Held by Equity Small-Cap Mutual Funds:	$409 billion[41]

Source: Morningstar; Investment Company Institute. 2013

Chart F: Households Owning Mutual Funds

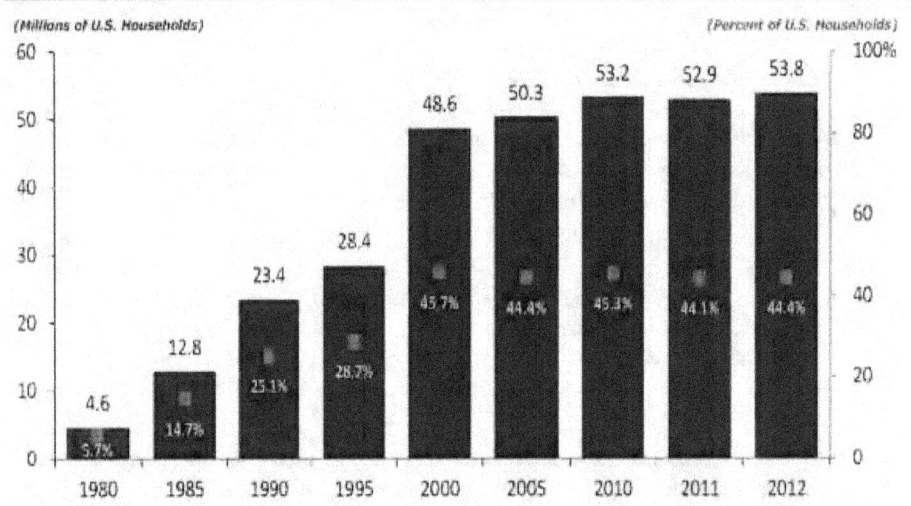

Source: Investment Company Institute. 2013[42]

Of course, millions of individual investors also participate directly in the equities market without institutional products like mutual funds or pensions. Some argue that these investors are the primary beneficiaries of the current market structure due to the lower transaction costs they now enjoy. However, the task force believes that this argument misses the bigger picture. According to CapIQ, retail investors own nearly 75 percent of all small-cap company[43] shares in the market. By and large, these investors own small-cap stocks because they aim to realize price appreciation over the long term as those companies grow. Unfortunately, for most small-caps, that price appreciation will be muted without the liquidity that only comes from robust institutional participation in the market. For this reason, the ECF Task Force believes that a more liquid

---

[38] Ibid.

[39] Investment Company Institute. 2013.

[40] Ibid.

[41] Morningstar. As of June 2013. "Small-cap" includes small value, small blend, small growth funds.

[42] 2013 Investment Company Fact Book: A Review of Trends and Activity in the Investment Company Industry. Washington, DC: Investment Company Institute. Available at www.icifactbook.org<http://www.icifactbook.org

[43] Defined as companies with market caps under $250 million.

small-cap market with greater participation by institutions will offer greater potential benefits to individual investors over the long term than **price improvement** on their trades.

Chart G: U.S. Equities Ownership & Trading Characteristics

	Sub $750 Market Cap	Above $750 Market Cap
Institutional Ownership	31.3%	83.3%
Retail Ownership	68.8%	16.7%
Research Analysts	2	14
30D ADTV	0.3 million shares	1.8 million shares
30D $ADTV	$2.0 million	$70.0 million

Source: CapIQ as of October 25, 2013. Includes all major U.S. exchanges.

Given the dynamics outlined above, the Equity Capital Formation Task Force believes that the current market structure is not adequately serving the needs of small-cap companies or the investors who wish to buy and sell their stocks. For this reason, this task force recommends developing and implementing new "rules of the road" for the trading of small-cap stocks. Specifically, public companies with market capitalizations of below $750 million should be quoted at minimum increments of five cents, and that they should trade at only the bid price, the ask price, or the mid-point between the two. The task force believes that these Small-cap Trading Rules (STaR) will foster a market structure for small-cap stocks that will provide for fundamental trading liquidity in these issues.

Unfortunately, there exists no method for testing or studying STaR's potential effects outside of the implementation of a program that can observe live trading over a significant period of time. Therefore, these rules should be implemented as part of a carefully considered, well-designed pilot trading program that limits its impact to small-cap stocks, tests the effects of STaR empirically over a significant time period, and enables the SEC to determine whether STaR should be implemented permanently for small-cap trading.

Detailed Recommendations:

2.1. The national exchanges should conduct a pilot trading program, overseen by the SEC, in which select small-cap companies trade under new Small-Cap Trading Rules (STaR). Under STaR:

   2.1.1. Participating companies will have market capitalizations below $750 million. The $750 million market cap criterion was selected by the task force to focus the benefits of STaR on only those companies that need them, without impacting market structure for the vast majority of the market. According to our research, a cap of $750 million will limit STaR's effects to only 2 percent of all trading volume on U.S. exchanges.[44]

   2.1.2. Participating companies should be quoted in minimum price increments of $0.05 and trade only at the bid, the offer or the mid-point between the two. Most of the analysis of current market structure has zeroed in on increasing minimum quote increments as the best option for mitigating the effects of the new market structure on the IPO and small-cap ecosystems. This theory posits that larger spreads will induce liquidity in small-caps, which in turn may eventually restore incentives for traditional aftermarket support. While this task force agrees with that assessment, its members also believe that widening minimum quote increments alone is not enough to affect all of the trading practices that currently inhibit small-cap liquidity.

---

[44] Bloomberg.

For this reason, the task force has included the trading stipulations outlined above. Under STaR, both institutional and individual investors can be matched at the increment. Institutions that internalize order flow will still be able to provide price improvement for individual investors, but only at the mid-point between the bid and offer. By limiting the number of increments at which a small-cap stock can trade to the bid price, the offer price or the mid-point between the two, STaR will eliminate sub-penny increments and create fewer total points at which a market participant with a customer order in hand can "step in front" of an order – thus reducing the incidence of this practice. In turn, this will encourage fundamental institutional investors and fundamental market makers to post more liquidity on their bids and offers.

2.2. **The SEC and the national exchanges should begin the process of designing and implementing the STaR pilot as soon as is feasible.** As mandated by the JOBS Act, the SEC studied and reported on the impact of smaller spreads and decimalization (collectively referred to as "tick sizes") on capital formation. However, after its review of academic literature, the SEC's report to Congress in July 2012 stated that further study was required to acquire the requisite data to draw a conclusion. During and since that time, the SEC has engaged in dialogue with the national exchanges on the possibility of developing an alternative market structure for small-cap trading. The Equity Capital Formation Task Force understands that this dialogue is ongoing, but this task force also believes that the time for taking action is now. That is because for each day that the U.S. small-cap ecosystem underperforms, Americans potentially lose innovative products and services, tax revenue and new jobs. Ultimately, the SEC must act as the final arbiter of the planning and implementation process. In this role, however, they must solicit and weigh input from all stakeholders in this process, as well as consider all relevant research and data that may inform the implementation plan.

2.3. **The STaR pilot design must include a clear methodology for collecting and analyzing data regarding STaR's effects on small-cap trading.** This methodology should measure the effects of STaR through analysis of the following metrics:

(a) **Relative level of trading liquidity.** Relative level of trading liquidity will be measured by any changes in the number of blocks traded (more than 5,000 shares), number of trades (absolute), displayed liquidity (quote) size, Average Daily Trading Volume, and single-name stock volatility.

(b) **Changes in institutional ownership.** Increases in institutional ownership would be desirable, both in number of institutions and as a percentage of ownership, because institutions generally provide higher trading volume.

(c) **Rate of equity capital issuance.** Higher rates of equity capital issuance would be a marker for lower costs of capital because issuers would resist issuing equity capital at depressed prices.

2.4. **The STaR pilot must run long enough to provide a true empirical test of STaR's effects on the small-cap market.** Under the pilot, STaR must remain in effect enough to allow for meaningful data capture and analysis across multiple business cycles and market environments. STaR must also remain in effect long enough to allow or encourage market participants to adjust their trading practices and/or business models to address potentially long-term market changes engendered by STaR. Otherwise, market participants may see less risk in simply "waiting out" the pilot, as opposed to changing their practices to capture or defend against resulting market effects.

2.5. **At the STaR pilot's conclusion, the SEC must use the empirical data generated by the pilot to evaluate whether Small-Cap Trading Rules should apply to small-cap trading on a permanent basis.**

Analysis

While the factors and market dynamics behind the changes in the U.S. equities market are complex, the underlying economic imperative is relatively simple. If we want investors to assume the risks and extra costs inherent in trading small-cap stocks, market structure must provide the potential for profit in doing so. The

Equity Capital Formation Task Force believes that larger minimum quote increment sizes and fewer price increments at which to trade will help produce this outcome. That's because the combination of these two important changes will allow for a simpler, more efficient market by enabling fundamentally oriented investors to more comfortably increase the posted size of their bids and offers while having to defend themselves less often against the practice of "stepping in front" by other market participants. Price improvement will still take place for a number of reasons, but it will do so at fewer and wider increments. As a result, the task force believes that these changes will encourage greater liquidity in small-cap stocks for investors.

Over time, the return of liquidity to the small-cap market may lead to a recovery of the aftermarket support system for small-cap stocks. With some of the economic incentives for small-cap trading restored, institutions may begin to invest resources in rebuilding their market-making and research functions. Research is a critical component of the information investors need to discover stocks, make informed investment decisions, and achieve positive outcomes. Yet, research can be scarce in today's market environment. In fact, nearly 29 percent of all exchange-listed companies have no "meaningful" analyst coverage of their stocks.[45] Among companies with market caps of less than $250 million, 55 percent lack meaningful coverage.[46] Put another way, investors cannot access meaningful analyst research on more than half of all micro-cap stocks.

For companies without meaningful analyst coverage, the consequences for long-term capital formation are significant. There is a causal relationship between high-quality analyst coverage and a stock that is widely held, actively traded and fully valued. Correspondingly, the absence of coverage can lead to low visibility among investors, limited liquidity and lower market valuation relative to peers.[47] This also results in higher illiquidity taxes paid by the individual investors who overwhelmingly own their stocks.

Chart H: Institutional vs. Individual Ownership of All U.S. Listed Stocks

Mkt Cap Range	Median		
	Market Cap	Institutional Ownership	Individual Ownership
$0M – 50M	$27.4	10.7%	89.3%
$51M – 100M	71.7	19.5	80.5
$101M – 250M	171.7	35.8	64.2
$251M – 500M	348.4	49.3	50.7
$500M – 1BN	712.8	70.0	30.0
$1BN +	3,448.3	84.0	16.0

Source: Data from CapIQ; methodology by Keating Investments.

In conclusion, the Equity Capital Formation Task Force believes that the combination of wider quoting increments and limited execution prices provided by STaR will bring back the fundamental institutional investors necessary to provide additional trading liquidity to small-cap stocks – and the positive equity capital formation that accompanies it. It must be noted that this task force does not make recommendations for changing market practices lightly. Nor is it suggesting that the market structure be changed for trading in

---

[45] Keating, Tim. Keating Investments. "Analyzing the Analysts: A Survey of the State of Wall Street Equity Research 10 Years after the Global Settlement." (January 2013). "Meaningful" is defined as having at least one analyst from the approximately 100 firms included on either the Institutional Investor or StarMine list of analyst rankings.

[46] Keating, Tim. Keating Investments. "Analyzing the Analysts: A Survey of the State of Wall Street Equity Research 10 Years after the Global Settlement." (January 2013).

[47] Ibid.

larger companies, where the bulk of the positive effects of decimalization are most prevalent. Again, the small companies that would be affected by STaR account for only 2 percent of all trading volume on U.S. exchanges.[48]

Small cap stocks account for only 2% of trading volume on U.S. exchanges.

That may seem like a small segment of the market on which to focus, but it is from where tomorrow's leading U.S. companies will grow. For this reason, market participants and policy-makers must seize this opportunity to nurture this critical ecosystem. Critics may argue that the need for such nurturing proves that many of these companies do not belong in the public market. Such an argument is short-sighted and unfair. Every small-cap company should have the opportunity to succeed or fail based on its fundamental performance and the willingness of long-term investors to provide it with capital for growth – not because the mechanics of how stocks are bought and sold today, versus 20 years ago, has changed. STaR will help restore that opportunity.

---

[48] Bloomberg

VII. The Road Ahead

America's capital markets work because they are fluid, dynamic, innovative and responsive. As stewards of these markets, we must embrace these same traits in our management of them. By acknowledging the issues outlined in the preceding sections, and by taking the recommended actions, this task force believes that market stakeholders will fulfill that responsibility. However, we must also see the bigger picture, and anticipate those roadblocks that lie beyond those we currently undertake to remove.

In this context, the Equity Capital Formation Task Force has identified two additional facets of the U.S. capital markets ecosystem that market participants and policy-makers will need to address in the wake of this report. These concern equities market research, and the regulatory landscape that emerging growth companies and other small-cap companies face – from the day they are founded to their daily operations in the public markets.

As described in the preceding market structure section, analyst research is a critical component of the information investors need to discover stocks, make informed investment decisions, and achieve positive outcomes. Yet the amount of research published by regulated, accredited research analysts and available to investors regarding many small-cap companies is insufficient for supporting requisite trading liquidity in those stocks. Recognizing the important role that equity research plays in the IPO process, the JOBS Act sought to address some of the limitations surrounding equity research for newly public companies. However, it did not change many of the rules governing liability in publishing research. As a result, the bar for publishing research remains high, so much so that many investment banks have decided that it is not worth the risk – especially where small-cap stocks are concerned. This situation has created an anomaly in the quality and flow of market information available to small-cap investors. In the absence of research from highly educated, highly qualified – and highly regulated – research analysts who work for broker-dealers, the majority of information available to small-cap investors now comes from unregistered, unregulated, non-accredited bloggers and other commentators who require only an Internet connection to fill the information void.

Regarding the regulatory landscape, the creation of the "emerging growth company" category and the "on-ramp" in the JOBS Act signaled the growing recognition among policy-makers of the need for scaled securities regulations, as opposed to a one-size-fits-all approach. However, these provisions are still exceptions to the rules – quite literally. They do not repeal any of the regulations that were steering promising young companies away from the public markets; they merely provide narrow and temporary relief from those regulations. Nor do they represent explicit mandates for future rulemaking – despite the encouraging precedent they provide. However, it does make sense to build on the precedent set by the JOBS Act and institute protocols that ensure that all new regulations take into account the specific capital formation needs and job creation abilities of EGCs. Simply put, regulations that are appropriate to impose upon large-cap companies like IBM and General Electric may create disproportionate burdens on emerging growth companies.

Granted, fully opening the on-ramp and fostering a more orderly flow of traffic on the public freeway require more immediate attention than the issues above. However, as we make progress on the latter, we must begin to look at how we can enable more companies to pursue IPOs, create jobs and grow in the public markets – where investors can participate in that growth. The ECF Task Force believes that the health of the research ecosystem and the flexibility of our regulatory approach can play direct roles in effecting these outcomes. The members of the Equity Capital Formation Task Force look forward to participating in that conversation.

VIII. Conclusion

As America's economy continues its slow but steady climb out of the Great Recession, the U.S. capital markets must once again lead the way by driving private sector job creation and growth. The Equity Capital Formation Task Force believes our system can do so, but only if it continues to provide America's most promising startups and small-cap companies with the public capital they need to grow, and continues to provide investors with the opportunity to participate in that growth.

As stewards of the markets and of the public interest, policy-makers have a responsibility to ensure that those markets remain fair and orderly, and that their benefits reach the largest number of Americans possible. This is especially critical now that so many Americans invest in the equities market as part of their retirement strategies. Congress and President Obama recognized this in 2012 when they enacted the JOBS Act, whose initial success has proved the efficacy of scaling regulations and reducing the risks and costs for emerging growth companies looking to going public. The Equity Capital Formation Task Force believes that policy-makers now have a critical opportunity to seize the momentum generated by the JOBS Act's success and apply its principles more broadly to benefit even more promising small companies – now and in the future. That's why the members of this task force stand ready to assist market participants and policy-makers in fostering dialogue regarding the issues addressed by this report, and in taking any actions that result from our recommendations.

By doing so, all of us can help refuel capital formation for America's innovative small companies. We can energize U.S. job creation and economic growth. And we can ensure that the road from innovative young startup to Fortune 500 Company and global leader continues to run directly through the U.S. capital markets.

IX. Appendices

Appendix A – Glossary of Key Terms

aftermarket: the trading of a stock between investors, subsequent to its IPO. Also called the secondary market.

emerging growth companies (EGCs): a new category of companies created by the JOBS Act. To qualify as an EGC, a company must have revenue of less than $1 billion in the most recent fiscal year, or a public float (excluding affiliates) below $700 million.

fundamentals: information about a company such as revenue, earnings, assets, liabilities and growth that analysts and investors use to value that company's stock.

individual investor: a person who buys and sells stocks for his or her personal account, as opposed to on behalf of an institution or other entity. Also known as a "retail investor."

initial public offering (IPO): a private company's first sale of stock to investors on the public market. Companies do this to raise capital for growth.

institutional investor: a business entity that buys and sells stocks on behalf of clients or itself. Institutions generally work with large amounts of capital and operate under fewer protective restrictions regarding trading activities than individual investors. Examples include asset managers, mutual funds, hedge funds, insurance companies and pension funds.

issuer: a company that has created shares of stock to sell to investors.

large-cap: shorthand for "large market capitalization" or a company/stock that meets the criteria. Large-caps are the biggest companies in the markets, with market valuations of above $5 billion to $10 billion.

market maker: a regulated broker-dealer firm that facilitates trading in a particular security by maintaining an inventory of that security, advertising buy and sell quotes for it, and trading from that inventory to fill or match orders.

position: ownership of a particular stock.

price improvement: offering/providing a better price at execution on a stock than the price quoted at the time of the order.

small-cap: shorthand for "small market capitalization" or a company/stock that meets the criteria. In this report, it refers to companies with market valuations below $1 billion.

tick size: the smallest increment at which the price of a stock is quoted. Stocks on the national stock exchanges trade at $0.01 minimum tick sizes.

trading liquidity: the ability of investors to buy or sell large blocks of a company's stock without materially affecting the price. This ability is affected by a number of factors, including market capitalization, trading volume, research coverage and visibility among investors.

Appendix B — Committee Details

About the Equity Capital Formation Task Force

Comprising professionals from across America's startup and small-capitalization company ecosystems, the Equity Capital Formation (ECF) Task Force formed in June 2013 to 1) examine the challenges that America's startups and small-cap companies face in raising equity capital in the current public market environment, and 2) develop recommendations for policy-makers that will help such companies gain greater access to the capital they need to grow their businesses and generate private sector job growth. The task force's efforts have been informed by discussions flowing from The Securities and Exchange Commission's Decimalization Roundtable (February 2013), which examined the impacts of decimalized pricing of securities on IPOs, trading, and liquidity for small and middle capitalization companies; and from the Capital Access Innovation Summit convened by the Treasury Department and the Small Business Administration in June 2013, which focused on the impact of the JOBS Act of 2012 on capital formation for emerging growth companies and what additional measures might benefit this process.

Members

We should note that the members of the task force listed below participated as individuals and not as representatives of their organizations. Thus, their input for this report and the positions contained herein do not necessarily reflect the views or positions of the organizations for which they work or are affiliated.

Issuers & Investor Relations:

- **Jeff Corbin**, CEO, KCSA Strategic Communications

- **Charles Crain**, Manager, Policy & Research, BIO

- **Kenneth Moch**, President & CEO, Chimerix, Inc.

Public Company Investors:

- **Cheryl Cargie**, Head of Trading, Ariel Investments

- **Kevin Cronin**, Global Head of Trading, Invesco

- **Jason Vedder**, Head of Trading, Driehaus

Venture Capitalists:

- **Jennifer Connell Dowling**, Senior VP Federal Policy, National Venture Capital Association

- **Timothy J. Keating**, President, Keating Investments

- **Scott Kupor**, Managing Partner, Andreessen Horowitz; Task Force Co-Chairman

Academicians:

- **Hal S. Scott**, Director, Committee on Capital Markets Regulation

Investment Bankers:

- **Carter D. Mack**, President, JMP Group Inc.

- **Tom O'Mara**, Co-Head of Equities, Cowen and Company

- **Jeffrey Solomon**, Chief Executive Officer, Cowen and Company; Task Force Co-Chairman

Securities Attorneys:

- **Jorge A. del Calvo**, Partner, Pillsbury Winthrop Shaw Pittman

- **Joel Trotter**, Partner, Latham & Watkins

Exchanges & Trading Organizatons:

- **Reagan Anderson**, Vice President, Government Affairs, NYSE Euronext

- **Terry G. Campbell**, Head of Global Government Relations, NASDAQ OMX

- **James Toes**, President & CEO, Security Traders Association

68

APPENDICES

Appendix C — Acknowledgements

The Equity Capital Formation Task Force wishes to express its gratitude to the following individuals, whose input and expertise contributed to the preparation of this report. Please note that their appearance on this list does not imply endorsement of this report or its recommendations.

Joshua Green, General Partner, Mohr Davidow Ventures; Chairman, National Venture Capital Association

William Heyman, Vice Chairman & CIO, Travelers; Former Director of the Division of Market Regulation, SEC

Stephen Holmes, General Partner, InterWest Partners; Member, SEC Investor Advisory Committee

Laura Cox Kaplan, U.S. Government, Regulatory Affairs and Public Policy Leader, PwC

Lawrence Leibowitz, COO, NYSE Euronext

Kate Mitchell, Partner, Scale Venture Partners; IPO Task Force Chair

John Stanley, Analyst, Cowen and Company

David Weild, Founder, Chairman, IssuWorks and Weild & Co.

Nancy Wu, Director, Cowen Group, Inc.

PREPARED STATEMENT OF ANDREW M. BROOKS
VICE PRESIDENT AND HEAD OF U.S. EQUITY TRADING, T. ROWE PRICE ASSOCIATES, INC.

JUNE 18, 2014

Introduction

Chairman Warner, Ranking Member Johanns, and distinguished Members of the Senate Subcommittee on Securities, Insurance, and Investment, thank you for the opportunity to testify today on behalf of T. Rowe Price[1] regarding the impact of high frequency trading (HFT) on the economy. My name is Andrew (Andy) M. Brooks. I am Vice President and Head of U.S. Equity Trading of T. Rowe Price Associates, Inc. I joined the firm in 1980 as an equity trader and assumed my current role in 1992. This is my 34th year on the T. Rowe Price trading desk.

T. Rowe Price, founded in 1937, is a Baltimore-based global adviser with $711.4 billion in assets under management as of March 31, 2014 and serving more than 10 million individual and institutional investor accounts.

We welcome the opportunity for discussion regarding the industry and market practices.

Since I last testified before this Committee in September 2012, we have seen considerable turnover in Congress, this Committee, and at the U.S. Securities and Exchange Commission (''SEC'', or the ''Commission''); however, there has been little change in addressing the issues discussed 21 months ago, although we do applaud the SEC's efforts in implementing limit up and limit down controls and developing the Consolidated Audit Trail. Additionally, we are encouraged by Chair Mary Jo White's recent comments suggesting a heightened focus on improving market structure and we appreciate this Committee's continued interest in improving our markets. However, order routing practices, payment for order flow, maker/taker pricing, market data arbitrage, and the myopic quest for speed are all issues that remain unaddressed. In addition, we have grown increasingly concerned about the growth of dark pools and the challenges of the direct ''fast'' feed operating alongside the ''slow'' Securities Information Processor (SIP) feed. We recognize that change in Washington is constant, but would like to emphasize the fact that the fundamental market structure issues we face as an industry are ever evolving and are incapable of being resolved without regulatory intervention.

Although this hearing is focused on HFT, we believe HFT is merely symptomatic of larger market structure problems. We are cautious not to lump all electronic trading into the class of HFT and further, we do not believe that all HFT is detrimental to the market. We are supportive of genuine market making; however, we acknowledge that there are predatory strategies in the marketplace that have been enabled by our overly complex and fragmented trading markets. Those parties utilizing such strategies are exploiting market structure issues to their benefit and to the overall market's and individual investor's detriment.

We question whether the functional roles of an exchange and a broker-dealer have become blurred over the years creating inherent conflicts of interest that may warrant regulatory action. It seems clear that since the exchanges have migrated to ''for-profit'' models, a conflict has arisen between the pursuit of volume (and the resulting revenue) and the obligation to assure an orderly marketplace for all investors. The fact that 11 exchanges and over 50 dark pools operate on a given day seems to create a model that is susceptible to manipulative behaviors. If a market participant's sole function is to interposition themselves between buyers and sellers we question the value of such a role and believe that it puts an unneeded strain on the system. It begs the question as to whether investors were better served when exchanges functioned more akin to a public utility. Should exchanges with de minimus market share enjoy the regulatory protection that is offered by their status as exchanges, or should they be ignored?

Additionally, innovations in technology and competition, including HFT, have increased market complexity and fragmentation and have diluted an investor's ability to gauge best execution. For example, in the race for increased market share, exchanges and alternative trading venues continue to offer various types of orders to

---

[1] T. Rowe Price Associates, Inc., a wholly owned subsidiary of T. Rowe Price Group, Inc., together with its advisory affiliates (collectively, ''T. Rowe Price''), had $711.4 billion of assets under management as of March 31, 2014. T. Rowe Price has a diverse, global client base, including institutional separate accounts; T. Rowe Price sponsored and sub-advised mutual funds, and high net worth individuals. The T. Rowe Price group of advisers includes T. Rowe Price Associates, Inc., T. Rowe Price International Ltd, T. Rowe Price Hong Kong Limited, T. Rowe Price Singapore Ltd., T. Rowe Price (Canada), Inc., and T. Rowe Price Advisory Services, Inc.

compete for investor order flow. Many of these order types facilitate strategies that can benefit certain market participants at the expense of long-term investors and, while seemingly appropriate, often such order types are used in connection with predatory trading strategies. We are supportive of incremental efforts, such as a recent initiative by the New York Stock Exchange to eliminate 12 order types from their offerings.

We also believe that increased intraday volatility over the past few years is symptomatic of an overly complex market. Though commission rates and spreads have been reduced, intraday volatility continues to be alarmingly high. It was refreshing to see a recent report from RBC Capital Markets[2] examining the impact of intraday volatility and exposing the high costs to investors. Most academics only look at close to close market volatility.

Increased market complexity results in a lack of investor confidence. Our firm is particularly focused on the interests of long-term investors although we appreciate the role other types of investors can have in creating a dynamic marketplace. A recent Gallup poll noted that American household ownership of stocks continues to trend well below historic norms.[3] One can never be sure what drives investor behavior, but it seems clear to us that we need to do a better job of earning investor's confidence in the market. Those investors who have stayed on the sidelines in recent years, for whatever reason, have missed out on significant equity returns. We worry that the erosion of investor confidence can undermine our capital markets, which are so important to the economy, job growth, and global competitiveness. Re-affirming a strongly rooted commitment to fairness and stability of the market's infrastructure is critically important.

Over the past two decades the markets have benefited from innovations in technology and competition. Generally, markets open at 9:30 a.m., close at 4:00 p.m., and trades settle efficiently and seamlessly. The markets function in an orderly fashion, but if one were designing a market from scratch we doubt that we would end up with the overly complex structure we have today.

Vibrant and robust markets function best when there are varied investment opinions, styles, and approaches. However, given the myriad of ways to engage in the markets, we feel that investors would benefit from an increased focus on market structure, particularly features that enable predatory and manipulative practices. We applaud looking into an enhanced oversight of HFT and other high frequency strategies and conflicts of interest in our current market structure. Disruptive HFT strategies are akin to a tax loophole that has been exploited and needs to be closed. Market participants utilizing such strategies are essentially making a riskless bet on the market, like a gambler who places a bet on a race that's already been run and for which he knows the outcome.

Suggestions

In the spirit of advancing the interests of all investors we might make the following suggestions:

A good first step might be to experiment with a number of pilot programs to examine different structural and rule modifications. We envision a pilot program where all payments for order flow, maker-taker fees, and other inducements for order flow routing are eliminated. We also envision a pilot that incorporates wider minimum spreads and some version of a "trade at" rule, which we believe would lead to genuine price improvement. These programs should include a spectrum of stocks across market caps and average trading volumes, among other factors. Additionally, we would advocate for a pilot program that would mandate minimum trade sizes for "dark pools." "Dark pools" were originally constructed to encourage larger trading interests and it seems perverse that many venues on the "lit" markets or exchanges have a larger average trade size than "dark pools".

HFT and market structure issues were recently brought into the public spotlight by Michael Lewis and his book *Flash Boys*.[4] Sometimes it takes a storyteller like Mr. Lewis to bring the attention needed to an issue, and we hope that all parties involved will come together and seize this opportunity to improve our markets. Again, we would advocate for pilot programs to test and ultimately implement measured yet significant changes. At the end of the day we are here because of our

[2] Bain, S., Mudassir, S., Hadiaris, J., and Liscombe, M. (2014). RBC Capital Markets, "The Impact of Intraday Volatility on Investor Costs: Insights Into the Evolution of Market Structure", RBC Capital Markets.

[3] "U.S. Stock Ownership Stays at Record Low". (n.d.). "U.S. Stock Ownership Stays at Record Low". Retrieved June 17, 2014, from *http://www.gallup.com/poll/162353/stock-ownership-stays-record-low.aspx.*

[4] Lewis, M. (2014). *Flash Boys: A Wall Street Revolt.* New York: W.W. Norton & Company, Inc.

firm commitment to all investors to ensure that the capital markets perform the functions for which they were designed-capital formation for companies and investment opportunities for both institutions and individuals.

On behalf of T. Rowe Price, our clients, and shareholders, I want to thank the Committee for the opportunity to share our views on how we can, together, make our markets as good as they can be.

ADDITIONAL MATERIAL SUPPLIED FOR THE RECORD

**ILLUSTRATIONS OF MINIFLASH CRASHES FROM MAY 13, 2014,
SUBMITTED BY CHAIRMAN WARNER**

Lorillard (LO), May 13, 2014

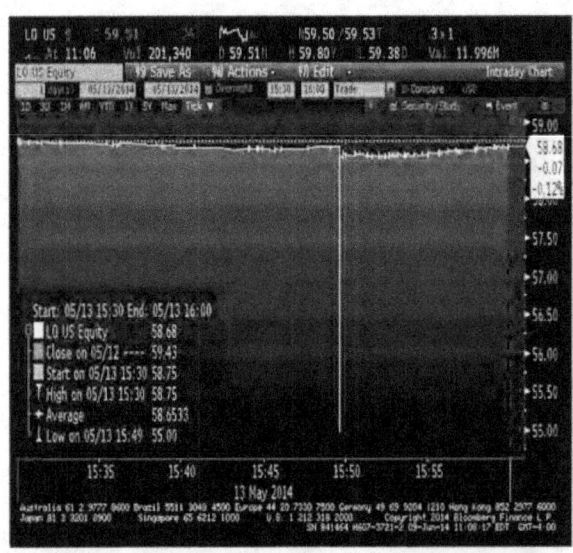

Xerox (XRX), May 13, 2014

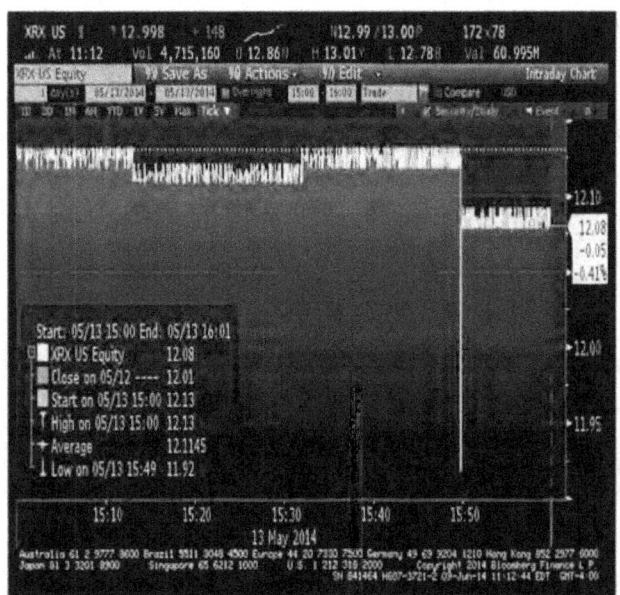

Nasdaq (NDAQ), May 13, 2014

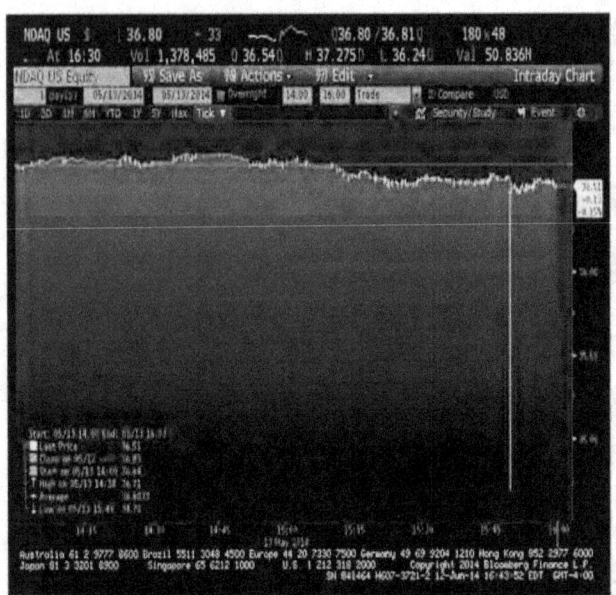

STATEMENT SUBMITTED BY GREG MILLS, HEAD OF GLOBAL EQUITIES DIVISION, RBC CAPITAL MARKETS

 **RBC Capital Markets**

RBC Capital Markets
Three World Financial Center
200 Vesey Street
New York, NY 10281

**Written Testimony of Greg Mills, Head of Global Equities Division,
RBC Capital Markets**

**To The
Subcommittee on Securities, Insurance, and Investment
Committee on Banking, Housing and Urban Affairs**

**For the Hearing on
"High Frequency Trading's Impact on the Economy"**

June 18, 2014

Chairman Warner, thank you for inviting RBC Capital Markets to submit testimony for today's hearing regarding the impact of high-frequency trading on the economy.

It is a privilege to present our testimony to you, Ranking Member Johanns, and the other distinguished members of this panel.

My testimony today is delivered on behalf of RBC Capital Markets, which is part of the investment banking platform of Royal Bank of Canada. RBCCM is a U.S. registered broker-dealer engaged in, among other things, providing equities trading and execution services to retail and institutional investors. These investors include large investment managers with trillions of dollars in assets under management. Those assets reside in employee pension funds and other vehicles that hold the savings of a great many individual investors. We work every day for our clients to successfully invest the hard-earned savings of millions of Americans – savings that those Americans put to work to build and grow businesses, to educate their children, and to prepare for a secure retirement.

My statement today makes two fundamental points:

First, that the evolution of U.S. equity market structure, including high-frequency trading – or "HFT" -- has produced significant benefits for market participants, but that predatory strategies associated with some forms of HFT have also imposed burdens -- on investors, public companies, and the overall economy; and

Second, that the ratio of benefits to burdens can be improved by making reasonable, focused reforms, including particularly to the so-called maker/taker pricing model that has become prevalent on many trading venues.

Let me now discuss these points in more detail.

At the outset, it bears emphasizing that the U.S. capital markets are among the world's deepest, most transparent, and most efficient. That result did not come about by accident. It is the result of ingenuity, entrepreneurship, and the work of policymakers and market participants to build a capital markets structure that serves the needs of investors, issuers, and the overall economy.

The question for policymakers and market participants today is not whether the markets today are liquid or illiquid, efficient or inefficient, transparent or opaque, fair or "rigged". Rather, the question is whether U.S. capital markets – as liquid, efficient, transparent, and fair as they are – can be even more liquid, more efficient, more transparent, and more fair. We would answer that question in the affirmative. And, indeed, we would respectfully submit that policymakers and market participants must continue to work to improve these markets in order for the markets to fulfill their vital role of supporting economic growth.

In that regard, we support the approach taken by SEC Chair White in her recent announcement of a series of "initiatives" to address "elements of today's market structure that work against the interests of investors and public companies." She has laid down a series of markers to begin to address concerns about market instability, high-frequency trading, fragmentation, broker conflicts, and market quality for small-cap firms. She has also stated her intention to proceed in a manner that is deliberate and data-driven.

RBCCM shares the view of Chair White and many others that the evolution of the U.S. equity markets has produced significant benefits for investors, issuers, and the economy as a whole. This evolution includes, but is not limited to, the growth of HFT. Starting in the late 1990's, a number of important changes began to occur in equity markets. These included amendments to the Order Handling Rules, specifically the Limit Order Display Rule and the Quote Rule, both of which improved price transparency; decimalization; other technological changes; Regulation NMS; and Regulation ATS, which promoted competition by allowing an exemption for ATSs from exchange registration requirements. These and other changes have all contributed to greater efficiency, liquidity, and transparency in the market relative to earlier times. HFT has helped bring about these improvements in equity market outcomes, but it is by no means the sole or primary driver of them.

Certain strategies using HFT can yield positive results for investors and issuers. Predatory strategies, however, may utilize HFT to exploit structural inefficiencies in the market and, combined with other market structure dynamics, contribute to negative outcomes such as inefficiency, opacity, and competitive imbalance.

In a recent study, we examined the intraday movements of 1800 stocks over a 17-year period. The study is unusual, if not unprecedented, in its depth and scope. We found that intraday volatility increased steadily in U.S. equities from 2001 to 2008, and has since remained at or near peak 2008 levels, after adjusting for broad changes in macro volatility[.]

This increased volatility is observable across the entire trading day, but is most pronounced during the morning session – when retail investors tend to be most active.

These trends have led to trades occurring at narrower displayed spreads, but further from fair value as measured by short-term volume-weighted average price.

Some argue that this data is actually a sign of market health because it shows the process of price discovery in a large and dynamic marketplace. Our study suggests a trade-off for narrow spreads that has been witnessed in the U.S. since the onset of decimalization, but the narrow spreads have been won through increased relative intraday volatility.

These findings suggest that competition among market participants leveraging speed across markets forms a type of feedback loop that increases everyday price volatility, and may contribute to increasing overall market volatility, including the types of "flash-crash" scenarios that have occurred in recent years. Several of the initiatives announced by Chair White in her June 5 remarks – including an anti-disruptive trading rule, dealer registration, required FINRA membership, better risk management and oversight of trading algorithms, and other potential measures to minimize consolidated data latency and other speed advantages – may help minimize some predatory HFT strategies.

However, we believe that additional steps may be necessary. The data from our study and others suggest that markets may be relying on liquidity providers that lack market incentives to maintain fair and orderly markets. In fact, the current equity market structure may actually offer adverse incentives to liquidity providers and others that have the effect of generating excess intermediation and short-term volatility.

One such adverse incentive is maker/taker pricing.

In her June 5th speech proposing reforms of equity market structure, Chair White discussed this pricing model and the negative incentives it can create. Maker/taker essentially is a pricing model that provides rebates or payments to providers, or "makers" of liquidity, and charges a fee to those who seek, or "take", liquidity. It is an outgrowth of the proliferation of trading venues over the past decade and a half, which has heightened competition among exchanges and other infrastructures to such an extent that these venues offer rebates to broker-dealers and other professional traders.

While we understand the history of and rationale for maker/taker pricing, it has perhaps inadvertently introduced a number of dynamics into the market that are inconsistent with the goals of transparency, efficiency, liquidity, and fairness.

First, maker/taker creates a potential conflict of interest between brokers and clients by incentivizing brokers to use routing that may be most cost-effective for them, but which may not be the best method of execution for their clients. As Chair White explained in her June 5th remarks, unless rebates and other forms of payments are passed through from brokers to customers -- a practice that may present significant operational challenges --

"they can create conflicts of interest [between brokers and their customers] and raise serious questions about whether such conflicts can be effectively managed."

Second, it reduces transparency by potentially distorting the price-discovery process. It does so by spawning a proliferation of rebates and fees that are opaque to many market participants, and that are not disseminated in displayed quotes. In so doing, maker/taker artificially narrows and widens displayed spreads but not actual spreads, because displayed spreads don't include access fees and rebates.

Third, maker/taker pricing has compromised efficiency and liquidity in at least the following ways:

• The length of exchange queues has increased, making it less likely for other market participants to provide passive liquidity with optimal execution;

• Passive market participants are forced to trade more aggressively to access liquidity;

• Liquidity is often fleeting – that is, it may disappear in times of market stress, particularly for less liquid, less widely known stocks; and

• Myriad order types, rebates, and fees proliferate as trading venues seek to capture market share, resulting in excessive fragmentation of order flow.

In her June 5th speech, Chair White proposed two initiatives to address maker/taker and payment for order flow more generally. The first is a rule to enhance order routing disclosures for large orders. In addition, she said she will request the exchanges to review their order types to ensure that they support fair, orderly, and efficient markets. Significantly, she also said that the Commission is considering additional measures, "including whether and how to further mitigate or eliminate potential sources of conflicts between brokers and customers."

One such additional measure would be to reform maker/taker pricing itself. We have joined with other market participants – including NYSE and a number of large institutional investors – to call for precisely this change on the grounds that it not only would mitigate or eliminate potential conflicts of interest between brokers and their clients, but it would also positively affect liquidity, transparency, and efficiency.

While we would prefer to see maker/taker replaced, we understand and support the SEC's data-driven approach to reform. To that end, we have proposed as a first step that the Commission conduct a pilot study of an alternative to maker/taker pricing. Such a study would, for a 6-month period, take 50 of the 100 most heavily traded U.S. stocks and, for those 50 stocks, prohibit the payment of rebates (or comparable inducements), and mandate that all venues where those stocks are traded be required to implement a rebate-free pricing structure.

The data from this pilot is likely to produce two sets of results. The first set would, in our view, demonstrate the aforementioned shortcomings of maker/taker pricing. Conversely, the second set of results would likely demonstrate the benefits of rebate-free pricing; that is, it would show that the incentive to initiate a transaction would be to profit from a move in the stock, not to collect rebates at the expense of other market participants.

In our view, the conclusion from both sets of data is likely to be that a rebate-free pricing structure will promote greater transparency, efficiency, and liquidity by eliminating the incentive to engage in rebate arbitrage. Further, it will reduce the likelihood of fleeting liquidity, mitigate potential conflicts of interest between brokers and their clients, and reduce market fragmentation caused by the proliferation of "rebate capture" order types created by exchanges.

In addition, we believe that, if implemented, this reform could result in reduced spreads and additional high-quality liquidity trading on displayed venues. This outcome would be a logical effect of significantly reduced exchange access fees, and accompanying positive order routing behavior of broker dealers (and other market participants) who currently incorporate access fees into their order routing processes. By narrowing the differential in access fees between many on- and off-exchange venues, we would anticipate less reliance on cost-effective routing, thereby incentivizing market participants to route orders based on the likelihood of an execution rather than on rebates or the avoidance of venues with high access fees. Trading with more desirable, more diverse order flow would likely offset any lost revenue by market participants who are accustomed to receiving a rebate for providing liquidity.

This scenario runs counter to the conventional notion that eliminating rebates would de facto result in wider spreads. In addition, while some participants have suggested that a reduction in exchange access fees must be coupled with a Trade-At rule, ostensibly to the benefit of increased exchange-routed orders, we would not necessarily agree. In fact, we anticipate more order flow moving from dark to lit venues under this proposed maker/taker reform, even without an additional Trade-At component, as lower access fees would naturally promote more on-exchange trading. Simply stated, lower access fees stemming from the elimination of rebates would have the greatest affect on exchanges – the exact venues charging the most to post and take liquidity.

The case for reform of maker/taker pricing is strong, and support for reform is building. Four of the five current SEC Commissioners have all said that maker/taker pricing deserves, at a minimum, further examination[2]. The Chairman of the NYSE has called for reform of maker/taker[3]. And a number of recent academic studies have reached a similar conclusion[4]. In our view, a pilot study on maker/taker pricing is a logical, modest, and data-driven step toward making U.S. equity markets more fair, transparent, liquid, and efficient.

Mr. Chairman, thank you again for the opportunity to provide testimony for today's hearing. We at RBC Capital Markets would be happy to respond to any questions that you, Senator Johanns, or other members of the Subcommittee may have. And we would be pleased to work with you, your colleagues, and your able staff to advance our shared goal of ensuring that our equity markets serve the interests of investors, companies, and the economy as a whole.

81

Footnotes

[1] "The Impact of Intraday Volatility on Investor Costs", May 2014, RBC Capital Markets

[2] SEC Chair Mary Jo White (June 5, 2014): "The cost to the broker for executing in different venues can vary widely. Some venues make payments directly to brokers as a means to attract particular types of order flow. These payments include the liquidity rebates paid by exchanges that use a "maker-taker" fee structure. They also include payments offered by off-exchange market makers to retail brokers for the marketable order flow of their customers. . . . When fees and payments are not passed through from brokers to customers, they can create conflicts of interest and raise serious questions about whether such conflicts can be effectively managed."
https://www.sec.gov/News/Speech/Detail/Speech/1370542004312#.U5XsllBdWxo

SEC Commissioner Kara Stein (February 6, 2014): "We should explore how the maker-taker pricing model impacts liquidity and execution quality. Does the current rebate system incentivize or penalize investors? I have heard from many investors, and even exchanges, who are worried about the incentives embedded in the current system, and if there are proposals to explore alternative approaches, we should consider them."
https://www.sec.gov/servlet/Satellite/News/Speech/Detail/Speech/1370540761194#.U0616iJDuxp

SEC Commissioner Luis Aguilar (April 2, 2014): "Of course, any comprehensive market structure review would require a close examination of the maker-taker model and any resulting conflicts between broker-dealers and their customers. To that end, one idea that the commenters have recommended is a pilot program in which maker-taker rebates would be temporarily prohibited for certain securities. The idea is that such a pilot program would allow the Commission and others to study the effects of the maker-taker model on order routing practices, transparency, and other metrics, and would help inform the discussion on whether the maker-taker model needs to be changed or eliminated. . . . I am hopeful that the Commission will take a serious look at this proposal and have requested the staff of our Division of Trading and Markets to devote time in the near term to this issue."
https://www.sec.gov/servlet/Satellite/News/Speech/Detail/Speech/1370541390232#.U062GtJDuxo

SEC Commissioner Daniel Gallagher (April 14, 2014): The "proliferation of 'maker-taker' must be revisited" as a part of a broader market structure review.
http://online.wsj.com/news/articles/SB10001424052702303887804579501881218287694

[3] Jeffrey Sprecher, Chairman and CEO of the IntercontinentalExchange, owner of the New York Stock Exchange (January 26, 2014) (speaking of maker/taker pricing): "Unfortunately it's spread throughout the equities markets in the U.S. and we can't unilaterally change it alone. But it's certainly something we want to raise the profile and start a conversation around because I think it hurts everybody in the market."
http://www.reuters.com/article/2014/01/27/intercontinentalexchange-nyse-sprecher-idUSL2N0L102V20140127

[4] *Maker-Taker Pricing Effects on Market Quotations*, Larry Harris (2013)
"This problem aggravates agency problems between brokers and their clients because most clients do not receive liquidity rebates or pay access fees. Accordingly, when brokers have discretion over the creation of order flow (for example, when designing algorithms), maker-taker pricing can distort their decisions. The maker-taker pricing can also distort trading decisions made by buy-side traders if rebates and fees go through the trading desk's account and are not passed back to the accounts to which the trades are assigned."
(http://www.lqg.org.uk/wp-content/uploads/2013/09/201309-Harris-Maker-taker-pricing-v0.9.pdf)

The Maker-Taker Pricing Model and Its Impact on the Securities Market Structure: A Can of Worms for Securities Fraud? Stanislav Dolgopolov (2014)
"In the absence of a pass-through mechanism, it is not difficult to see that brokers have the dual incentive to route liquidity-making orders to trading venues with higher rebates and, analogously, liquidity-taking

orders to trading venues with lower or zero fees." Maker/taker pricing "may also provide an additional incentive to internalize liquidity-taking orders or sell this order flow to internalizers/wholesalers." (http://papers.ssrn.com/sol3/papers.cfm?abstract_id=2399821)

Can Brokers Have it all? On the Relation between Make Take Fees & Limit Order Execution Quality
Robert Battalio, Shane Corwin, Robert Jennings (2013)
"Limit orders routed to venues with high take fees suffer greater adverse selection costs – they are more likely to trade when the price moves against them and are less likely to trade when prices move in their favor. This suggests that brokers routing limit orders to venues with the highest take fees (and make rebates) might not be obtaining best execution for their clients."
(http://www3.nd.edu/~scorwin/documents/BattalioCorwinJennings_20131213_SSRN.pdf)

Shall We Haggle in Pennies at the Speed of Light or in Nickels in the Dark? How Minimum Price Variation Regulates High Frequency Trading and Dark Liquidity
Robert Bartlett, Justin McCrary
"Our findings are robust to changes in stock exchange fee structures at the $1.00 cut-off, although maker/taker fee structures are shown to impair market quality both above and below this price point in certain contexts."
(http://www.utexas.edu/law/wp/wp-content/uploads/centers/clbe/bartlett.pdf)